COMMONSENSE PARENTING

Raising Principled Children in an Ever-Shifting Culture

Sarah K. Mwania, Jerry W. David,
& Shirley M. David

BROOKSTONE
PUBLISHING GROUP
Birmingham, Alabama

Brookstone Publishing Group
An imprint of Iron Stream Media
100 Missionary Ridge
Birmingham, AL 35242
IronStreamMedia.com

Library of Congress Control Number: 2022912423

Cover design by twoline || Studio

ISBN: 978-1-949856-75-0 (paperback)
ISBN: 978-1-949856-76-7 (ebook)

1 2 3 4 5—26 25 24 23 22

To our spouses, Al, Susan, and Solo.
Their names are not on the front cover,
but their wisdom, support, and
encouragement while writing
this book were invaluable.

Contents

When you are dead, you do not know you are dead. All the pain is felt by others. The same thing happens when you are stupid!

—Unknown

Introduction

One day, my daughter Sarah called my wife, Susan, and I with a real problem. Several of her young children were waking in the middle of the night and disturbing her and her husband's sleep (as well as the sleep of others in the house). After several weeks of this loss of sleep, Sarah and Solo were way too tired to even think of a possible solution to this now overwhelming issue. After they tried everything they could think of—stopping daytime naps, no drinks before bed, long talks at night setting the ground rules not to "get up out of that bed," earlier bedtimes, then later bedtimes—she finally called us, desperate and tired!

Our initial response was, "Hey, you had those children, you figure it out" (ha-ha), but as we talked, we discovered Sarah and Solo had been allowing the kids to come into their bed. Well, simple solution. I told Sarah, "When they come in, just have a pallet—and not too comfortable a pallet—and simply tell them they are not allowed in your bed, but they can lay on the floor."

Within days, Sarah and Solo were ecstatic to report that this idea worked for most of the kids, but the problem was still not fully solved. A couple of the kids were actually happy to sleep on the floor. This time, I said, "I'm out of ideas. Call your grandmother."

My mother, who we all think is a bit of a seer and one of the best creative parents we have ever encountered, offered the following advice after listening to the problem.

She instructed Sarah to put a new toy they really liked on top of the fridge, and a small calendar with two weeks of check-off marks on the front of the fridge. If they went two weeks without getting out of bed, they got the toy. If they went eight days without getting out of bed, but then on the ninth day got out of bed, then the calendar was reset and another two weeks would be clocked before the toy was released to the child. Her plan worked, and Sarah and Solo got the rest they needed and deserved.

Problems like this arise all the time in families with young children. Maybe you're tired, like many young parents, or maybe you're so close to the forest you can't see the trees. When you're in the thick of things, it's sometimes hard to see or grasp a simple commonsense solution to an overwhelming problem. As I watched my children deal with their children, I realized a book describing basic child-rearing principles employed by three generations of parents would be useful. A book that provides some commonsense solutions to problems parents everywhere might be facing, today or in the future.

Maybe you don't have anyone to call for help or advice, but through these pages and the stories offered from different generational perspectives, I hope this book will bring hope, encouragement, and yes, even a commonsense solution to your role as a parent.

Not Another Parenting Book

I know, I know. Right now you're probably wondering, "Why does the world need another parenting book?" I couldn't agree more. My daughter Sarah has produced and published a triweekly video blog called *Our Tribe of Many* over the past four years, where viewers are given a glimpse into her large family and the daily routines of life and raising children.

Along the way, I've been astonished to see the plethora of questions and comments she receives about her family of thirteen. As she thoughtfully answers each one, I see her subscriptions growing beyond her wildest imagination. Many have asked how she and her husband, Solo, do it. Others have offered very complimentary remarks, while still others have questioned her sanity.

In a very real sense, I can understand all the various responses. But so often the ones that really catch my attention are the serious inquires with regard to raising this large family. Reading those comments and questions has made me aware that many people do not realize that raising children, whether one or eleven, is not a hit-or-miss proposition. Sarah and Solo raise their children without fear or intimidation because of the previous generations who had implanted certain life principles about home, family, and children. These ideals became a natural part of their approach to all things regarding parenting. In other words, Sarah is a product of her upbringing, just as I was a product of mine.

The video blog, along with my years of pastoral service in Lincoln, Nebraska, and hundreds of counseling sessions with concerned parents trying to raise children to the best of their ability, made us understand how a book on parenting with the perspective of three separate generations could be a very real benefit to so many.

Common sense. That phrase is listed in the dictionary as a noun representing "sound practical judgment that is independent of specialized knowledge, training, or the like; normal native intelligence."[1] I like that—normal native intelligence. Sounds like it's available to just about everyone. Yet it is one of the most overlooked concepts in our culture.

Right now there is such an emphasis on specialized knowledge and contextualized approaches to everything in life. When you add other paradigms such as political correctness, avoidance of even sneezing lest you offend, and other societal bents too numerous to list here, you can begin to quickly approach decisions, perceptions, and instructions without any relation to basic common sense. You can almost hear the lexicographers bemoaning the lack of *normal native intelligence* in their definition. In fact, the origin of the term *common sense* is from the fourteenth century and has its meaning in the power of mentally uniting the impressions conveyed by the five physical senses, thus "ordinary understanding, without which one is foolish or insane."[2]

When approaching the very important skill of parenting, I remain pretty much blown away with the total lack of common sense that is exhibited these days, even by people who practice common sense in so many other areas of their life. Now, before I move too far down the road, let me give an important disclaimer at the beginning of this book. I'm not a psychologist, therapist, or clinician. I'm just a parent and former pastor who has witnessed a lot of stupidity in parenting, even some on my part. That's why my son-in-law, when I began writing this book, sent me the quote that's at the beginning of this introduction. I'm not a perfect parent or pastor, for that matter. I've made quite a number of mistakes in both areas—stupid mistakes. If I were given the chance to redo some decisions, I would most certainly take the initiative.

However, when I have thought about both my upbringing and my parenting of my two children, I'm convinced the times that shaped me most and resulted in any success were those situations, unusual circumstances, or just everyday parenting experiences accompanied by a heavy dose of common sense.

I've wanted to write a book on parenting for a long time now, and over the years I've gathered my thoughts and scribbles in a file for such an opportunity. I wanted to title it *Raising Children Is a Mind Game*. I've always thought my parents parented me this way—straightforward, honest, and without complication—and certainly I raised my two this way. In other words, my parents didn't just think they were smarter than us; they knew it, so nothing we did or said intimidated them as parents. That doesn't mean playing tricks. It just means employing the common sense that we have as adults, and that children haven't acquired yet!

But just before I began to write, I recognized the book would be infinitely more interesting if I asked my mother and my daughter to help. So, although I'm literally putting the words on paper, the wisdom is coming from all three of us. As an extra bonus, I have incorporated their creative and wise input and experiences in each chapter. After all, you can't really tell if you enjoy any success in parenting until you examine the grandchildren (that third generation). My parents, Al and Shirley, raised four children—Jerry, Ron, Mike, and Nannette. Each of those children raised children, and now those children are raising their children. It's fun to watch and be a part of such a heritage. And like any family, we have our stories, history, successes, and mistakes.

In this book, we want to cover just seven of the most important concepts we consider crucial to good parenting, and we're going to do so through story, basic principles, and a good dose of common sense. But please note: these principles don't guarantee success. There are too many variables for that, including the fact that each child has been given free will by his or her Creator. They get to exercise that will, in spite of any training, instruction, or example a parent might provide.

We recognize we may offend some people with this commonsense approach, but ask that if you read something that seems offensive at first blush, sit back, take several deep breaths, and think it through a bit before letting the offense escalate. We'll bet in most cases you'll come to the point of not just agreeing with us (that's not our goal, by the way) but discovering a little common sense is going to make your life a lot easier as a parent. Additionally, we think someday your children will end up employing the same commonsense principles when it comes time to raising their children. That's how successive and successful generations are produced.

Let me conclude this introduction by telling you what I've told countless couples and parents over decades of pastoring and parenting: If you didn't have good parents, and you didn't come from a loving or caring home, and if you now think you are not equipped for this complex thing called "parenting," let me dispel that lie right now. You can begin a whole new paradigm, a whole new archetype. And one day a child, grandchild, or even great grandchild is going to look back and thank you for being such a commonsense parent.

Whether you are a Christ-follower or not, you have a loving God on your side who wants to make you successful in everything you touch, particularly in the family arena. In fact, God established family and family lines and offers His commonsense instructions throughout the Bible. We will quote the

Bible many times in this book, but there's more for you if you'll take the time to investigate His Word yourself.

Enjoy,

As parents, our ultimate purpose isn't simply to give our children food and shelter for the first twenty years of life. Our purpose is to one day present to the Lord, the church, and the world mature young adults who are good servants, good stewards, and good citizens.

—Randy Alcorn

CHAPTER ONE

"Becoming the Perfect Parent—Not!"

Planting Trees and Carving Pillars

Parenting 101

I remember like it was yesterday, even these forty-two years later. We had just arrived home from the hospital with our first child, Sarah. We only lived about five or six blocks from the hospital, but I drove very slowly and deliberately so as to avoid all potholes and any potential accidents. I do remember blowing my horn at a couple of—in my new-parent opinion—reckless drivers who were not paying attention. Didn't they know I had a newborn on board? What were they thinking?

When we arrived home, I carried Sarah inside, carefully, in her car seat. Then, I got Susan unloaded and into the house along with everything we were given at the hospital to start out this parenting gig with at least some sort of jump start: diapers, a bathtub, all sorts of creams, and other sundry items.

After we all got settled, I lay down on my back on the couch and laid Sarah—all nine-plus pounds of her—across my chest on her belly. That's when it hit me, and hit me hard!

I was ultimately responsible for this new life placed in my care, and this was not going to just be a good game of playing house. I was responsible! Tomorrow morning when I awoke, I would be responsible. Five, ten, even fifteen years from now, I would still be responsible. I would have had to take to my bed for a week if I'd thought beyond that.

I was responsible to feed, clothe, nurture, discipline, train, school, protect, guide, instruct, provide for, and comfort this new human being for a very long time. I was now a "parent." What were we thinking when we thought it'd be cool to have children?

I had never been so totally petrified or terrified in my entire life. When I took an internal inventory of my various skill sets, my good looks, my education, my bank accounts, my current job, and the little bungalow we were living in, the inventory showed a glaring deficit. I have to be honest. My first thought was *Let's give it a week and see how to all goes, and if it doesn't work, we can return her.* To where, I had no idea.

The term *parent* landed on my head with a weight and a thud that I hadn't ever anticipated. I knew I couldn't let Susan know how terrified I was, because that would only upset her, but inside my nerves were in a state of high alert and I felt on edge. I should have thought to take my pulse, as I probably would have ended up back at the hospital myself.

And speaking of the hospital . . . they didn't help much either. The night before Susan and Sarah were released to come home, it was the hospital's tradition to take away the baby and wheel a silver cart with a beautiful steak and lobster dinner into our room. All was served on silver, with the finest china and beautiful cutlery, along with crystal glasses. I remember thinking at the time, "I could get used to this. A romantic dinner with my wife every night, someone taking care of the child, and a lit candle flickering between us. No noise, no confusion, no problem, no responsibility!"

The first night home, Susan and I were both up with a screaming child most of the night. Where were the nurses? Where was the steak? Where was the candle? Alas, just a memory at this point, and the only way to get that back was to have another child. No way, not at this point!

I think it was John Steinbeck, the noted author, who said, "It takes courage to raise children." I couldn't agree more with John.

I thought this thing called parenting was going to be a cakewalk. I mean, after all, we had a dog, and how hard was that? My parents seemed to do okay, although I knew I would be so much better at this parenting thing than they were, and had known this really since I was about fourteen. Now, it was time to regroup and rethink this whole thing, and I had better come up with a plan that would carry me through at least the next twenty years.

There isn't a parent in the entire universe who doesn't start out parenting with the goal of having at least an equal, if not better, parent/child relationship than what they'd experienced as a child growing up. And there isn't a parent in the world who doesn't hope, at the beginning, that the newborn child will grow strong, mature gracefully, and become someone who gets to realize all his or her hopes and dreams.

The Two Main Premises of Our Three Generations

As we begin this journey about the very important and often misunderstood concept of parenting, I want to state two distinct premises that have guided all three generations of Davids when it has come to our own parenting. Both premises are taken from the Bible, and although that fact is not intended to make us sound preachy or cause the reader to think the three of us are standing in some exalted and sanctimonious position, these two premises have impacted us the most, and that fact must be shared at the beginning.

The first premise states that God's ways are perfect and His promises *always* prove true (Psalm 18:30). Now, although there are plenty of examples of the Bible calling us to perfection, we kid ourselves if we think we can be perfect in this parenting arena right out of the gate. In fact, there's a pretty old saying that serves as a great measuring tool regarding each of our parenting skills. It's said you never know how good of a parent you have been until there are grandchildren that can prove out your parenting skills.

In my case, it was only by the grace of God, some good common sense, and some great family and friends' support that we were even able to get through our parenting years with children and be happy we went ahead and did the parenting "gig."

The second premise is found in Psalm 144:12–15 (ESV). This passage gives a great goal for all of us as parents to work toward. "May our sons in their youth be like plants full grown, our daughters like corner pillars cut for the structure of a palace" (v. 12). Simply put, I think of parenting as planting trees and carving pillars. That powerful word picture provides for us a real and tangible goal of what we want to see produced in our children. Something to aim for. We all need something to aim for, don't we? If we don't have that, we leave things to chance, and that hardly ever works out well.

This scripture helped Susan and me to set as our goal to raise sons and daughters who would not be followers but leaders. It really didn't matter to us what they would do with their lives, but that their lives would be lived honorably, with purpose, and with a deep sense of personal fulfillment. The other thing I wanted, like the generations before me, was to raise children who learned for themselves how to rightly parent their children, resulting in a lineage we would all be proud of.

The First Thing to Remember

Right off the bat, every parent needs to understand that no matter how many nice scripture verses, best intentions, and support and advice you might enjoy from parents, grandparents, friends, neighbors, and the postman (since everyone has an opinion), you will never achieve perfection when it comes to raising children. Why? Because you aren't perfect in this world, and your children aren't either. They are unique, and no two are alike in personality, talent, or emotion.

Sarah Says

When I was pregnant with my first child, my aunt, who had ten children herself, had given me a book to read about getting babies to sleep well through the night. I read that book and even studied it at her recommendation. I had a good plan going into my first, very own newborn. And it worked!

The formula I loosely applied did the trick. Judah was sleeping eight hours in a night by six weeks old, and twelve hours a night a month later. Of course, I repeated this tactic with my next seven children. Isabelle, Luka, Micah, Victory, Eli, Noelle, and Hope all came along and slept fantastically. Just as the book had promised! As you can imagine, at that point I thought myself a baby-sleep expert. I would not say that out loud . . . but I was quick to offer tips to other parents who were struggling in the sleep department. Sleep is so important! And I inwardly wondered why my advice would not work for some parents. Maybe they were applying it wrong? Maybe they did not apply it at all?

Then I had Destiny. Oh, boy . . . or rather girl . . . my sweet, darling Destiny. I brought her home from the hospital and immediately knew something was different. She cried all night that first night! She would not let me put her down. What in the actual world? None of my own tips or tricks made a difference for this child. She slept on her very own schedule. She did a whole lot of things her own way, in fact!

I quickly learned my lesson. I was not, in fact, a sleep expert for infants. Instead, I now had a lot of grace for parents who were walking around in a sleepy daze. As in most areas of parenting, the more children I have, the less I know. Every child is different! What works for one—or even eight—may not work for another. Seth came along later and had sleeping habits very similar to Destiny's. I was no longer shocked. I was humbled. Our children don't need parents with all the answers. They need parents to care for them and their needs. You are the perfect parent for the children God gave you—imperfections and all. Now I'm pretty certain that anyone who has it all figured out in any one area of parenting probably just has not had enough children!

Second, we live in an imperfect world, and whether we realize or not, we are fighting as parents against a tremendously powerful influence of a world that doesn't share our same perspective or values. The struggle really seems like a war at times, just trying to keep the imperfect world on the outside of our home. The problem with keeping that world outside is that we don't stay cooped up in our homes all our lives. We have to leave our homes and live in the world.

So pursuing the perfection game, which many try, will only lead to disappointment, heartache, and even a sense of failure. Besides, who's to say what is perfect? If polled with that question, we would never achieve any kind of consensus.

Again, everyone has an opinion, as you find out quickly when you have your first child.

Because of this, when you read parenting books that offer you a very precise and prescribed way or formula to raising children, you might want to save your money. What you will find works for one child will not usually work for the rest. You don't need a formula as much as you need some basic principles that are nonnegotiable to you, along with a good dose of flexibility.

Remember, this parenting thing isn't a sprint; it's a long-distance marathon. You need to pace yourself. You need to have confidence in yourself. And you need to be ready to change your parenting approach on any number of different paradigms, quickly.

The Parenting Sacrifice

I suppose we've all observed parents who still act like children—sometimes to the point where you can't tell who is the child and who is the adult. When I see that kind of behavior, I shake my head and breathe a quick prayer for the children. Life is going to be a bit of a harder road for them.

If you haven't figured it out already, parenting requires a sacrifice. You feel it, your spouse feels it, even the family dog will experience a level of unanticipated sacrifice soon after that new baby is brought home from the hospital. While the dog can sulk and ignore the baby, or worse, a parent cannot. That baby knows what she wants and when she wants it, and you'd better not delay or she'll really let you know her displeasure.

Shirley Says

My husband and I are now over ninety years old, and if we were given a second chance to raise a family again, there are so many instances where we would have done things differently. Looking back, it's a bit shocking to us that, in spite of our mistakes, our children all grew into very responsible adults, and we are so proud of each of them.

They all chose their mates carefully and were attracted to those who were raised with similar values.

So now for us, the end of the story is getting close, and we now have twelve grown grandchildren who have families of their own and, at the latest count, we have thirty-one great-grandchildren!

Now, with no overt parenting responsibility, we are able to sit back and enjoy all of them, as they pursue their own life goals and raise their families.

And to answer the question you may be asking yourself right now, "Was it worth it?" I can only answer with a resounding ABSOLUTELY!

It goes without saying that parenting *requires* personal priorities and goals adjustments. Those lofty ideas of sons like full-grown plants and daughters like palace pillars don't stand a chance just because you hoped for the best and crossed your fingers. Parenting involves work and is a full-time commitment. Please don't make a mistake in thinking here.

This aspect is one of the things that gave me a greater appreciation for my own parents. Susan and I had two children. My parents had four. I don't know how they handled three boys and one girl. Raising just one girl and one boy usually left me with my tongue hanging out and panting by the end of most weeks. And as they got older, the work intensified, which was another shock to my system. I found out feeding a baby a bottle at all hours and changing diapers all the time was easy compared to helping a teenage son and daughter decide what learning track they want to take in high school that will prepare them for what they think might be their future career. And don't even get me started with the challenges of dating, hormones, and marriage!

Why is this subject of sacrifice so important? Because it's one of the first principles overlooked in our current culture by new parents. Let me explain. Earlier generations handled children a bit differently. The culture just two generations before mine put a lot more emphasis on traditional (for that time period of history) roles for the parents. Dad went to work, and Mom—no matter the giftings or talents she possessed— sacrificed and stayed at home to raise the children. But don't mistakenly think Dad didn't sacrifice, because many, including my own father, worked two full-time jobs to provide for his family. When I think about it, there were a number of fathers in the neighborhood where I grew up that did the exact same thing.

Additionally, in previous generations, families weren't nearly as separated as they are now. The world has grown a lot smaller and we will often find our extended families (parents, siblings, grandparents, great-grandparents, aunts, and uncles) all over the globe. So the emotional and physical support previous generations would enjoy by having family nearby is almost gone or nonexistent today.

Additionally, statistics show there are a lot more single-parent families now, which typically makes the level of sacrifice greater on one individual. However, the mindset that our current culture has produced—for good or bad—places the desire for self-fulfillment as the top priority. If this mindset is not recognized and addressed, parents will usually see children as a hindrance to their own fulfillment and will resent the sacrifice of any part of themselves or their lifestyle.

I think everyone can agree that children raised without active parent participation, or with mere "figurehead" parents, will be severely challenged as they grow and develop. One of the best ways we learn is by imitating role models in our lives, and our parents (sometimes singular) are the first and best role models we look to—whether that model is negative or positive.

Think about it. When you bring that child into the world and hold him or her in your arms the very first time, you think of all the things you can say and do to influence him or her. Being a parent is a tremendous responsibility and requires a tremendous sacrifice. What you do with that little child can influence not only him or her but everyone they meet. And not only for a day or a month or a year but for a lifetime. Just remembering that reality makes the sacrifice I need to make much easier to understand and, ultimately, enjoy.

There is a sacrifice of not only our priorities and goals as parents when raising children but also of our time and finances. I honestly couldn't believe the demands on my time that having a child in the home made on me. I find real enjoyment in reading, and when I would find a moment to sit down in a quiet place to read, inevitably there was something that would keep me from doing so, or that would interrupt once I started. I can assure you, it wasn't the dog!

Running children to this school event, that piano lesson, another church activity, a sports happening, and . . . well, this list goes on and on and on . . . required a sacrifice of time from someone, usually me or my wife. And to pay for all the above meant I would probably be sacrificing the little money I'd set aside to treat myself to a Big Mac meal at the end of the week. Do you know how much piano or violin lessons cost? And it's particularly grating to pay out all that good money when, for the first two years or so whenever the "gifted" child picked up the violin to play, it made a noise similar to a cat getting their tail crushed by a moving rocking chair.

Sarah Says

Parenting is the number-one sacrifice Solo and I have ever made. It is daily. Hourly. Sometimes the sacrifice seems to be every moment when you just want to sit in silence with your feet up and drink an iced tea, uninterrupted. Parenting is not for the weak at heart. You tell your toddler no and have to get up to redirect. Then it happens again. And again. And again. And again! At this point, you are tempted to give up, but, oh no. Give up now and you will be dealing with the same behavior tomorrow and *forever*. So you get up and redirect one last time. Success!

Always, we have found that making the sacrifice of our time, money, patience, and even what sometimes feels like our sanity produces so much more than what we could imagine. The sacrifice may feel great, but the result is always greater. Letting our kids help in the kitchen while they are young, messy, and highly motivated makes them confident and happy to help in the kitchen later in life, when they are actually helpful! Correcting the toddler for the twenty-fifth time trains your little one so that the next day you are no longer dealing with that same behavior. No worries, though, there will be a new one! We often ask ourselves, how will this behavior look at age five? Or fifteen? Or fifty-five? I have met people who are over fifty-five and never dealt with some behaviors that could have . . . no, *should* have probably been dealt with back in grade school. The sacrifices made now are *so* worth it. Think about things in your life that mean the most to you. I guarantee you, they did not come without some measure of sacrifice on your part. Every sacrifice made of your time, energy, and efforts is worth it when it comes to parenting. It is a lifelong commitment, but it is worth it!

Here's the thing you need to know. Parenting isn't something you sign on for six months, six years, or sixty-six years. Being a parent is a lifetime commitment and investment into people you love and whom you call your own. Remember, children are educated or raised more by what the grown-up (read: parent) is, and not by his or her talking and instructing. It is a job that only offers a hands-on and on-the-job level of preparation. You are not born a parent and naturally gifted in this area. You are not sent to school and educated in an advanced degree of parenting. Oh, and you can't produce children and expect someone else to take on the responsibility of raising them. Sorry.

When you're in your eighties and your children are breaking into their sixth decade of living, they will still remain your child. The responsibility of that does not diminish; it only morphs into a position where you are doing much less instruction (if any) and much more praying to God on their behalf. And according to those who know, that is the most powerful position any parent can find themselves in.

After all, God is the only parent who has ever been perfect.

Commonsense Applications
- What was your perspective on parenting prior to becoming a parent? What immediate insight, if any, did you gain when you finally became a parent?
- Have you subconsciously pursued the "perfect parent" role for yourself? How's that working out for you?

- What sacrifices have you had to make that you were unaware you were going to have to make in your role as a parent?

Honor your father and your mother, so that you may live long in the land the Lord *your God is giving you.*
—Exodus 20:12 NIV

CHAPTER TWO

"What Goes Around Comes Around"

The Principle of Honor

Honor Your Father and Mother

"What goes around comes around." I think this is one of the first phrases I remember hearing my father repeat, and often. It was the mantra he seemed to live by. When something would go wrong and not according to plan, he'd say, "What goes around comes around." When someone would cheat him or slight him, he didn't get mad. He just exclaimed, "What goes around comes around." When he was dishonored somehow, "What goes around comes around."

As a police officer for many years in Detroit, this was one of my father's tricks for dealing with disrespectful and dishonoring people he encountered all the time. I think it was his way of cursing his enemies and those who meant to harm him or his family. It was almost as if he knew it was useless to waste his time and energy on teaching others how not to be stupid! However, this simple idea was also the underlying mantra given the place of honor in our home. My father was convinced, and convinced us, that if you dishonor someone, that grievance would always return to you somehow. You would find yourself being dishonored in return.

There was no room in our home for dishonor. We couldn't dishonor our parents, we couldn't dishonor other leaders and authorities in our lives, and we weren't allowed to dishonor other people, no matter their age, race, or gender. Not only would punishment be meted out if my dad heard any of us doing that, but in a greater way we feared our being in some way dissed ourselves. When I think about it now, I cannot ever remember my father dishonoring any of his children. Oh sure, he was often disappointed in us and our behavior or frustrated that we weren't living up to our potential, but we never heard the words "You're stupid" or "You'll never amount to anything." In fact, the opposite was true. He often told us, "You are a David and, therefore, you are a leader, so act like it." In other words, "Don't dishonor yourself!"

This principle is the first of seven in this book for a specific reason. Without a doubt, family works the best, as does our society, when we operate within an atmosphere where honor is the prevalent ingredient in our relationships. Honor is not only showing great respect and high esteem to someone in authority in our lives, but it finds its truest meaning when we defer to another or esteem another more highly than ourselves. Also, make no mistake, honor has that "what goes around comes around" paradigm about it.

Right now, even as we write this book, our society and culture are awash in an atmosphere of dishonor. If someone doesn't agree with us, dishonor them. If someone cuts us off on the freeway, dishonor them back. If I don't like the way I've been treated or "respected," then dishonor that one who treated me that way by mistreating them or noticeably showing them a lack of respect. But living in this way will only create a vicious cycle, leaving each individual at the center of a very small universe. Seems to all three of us that there's a lot of energy being expended just to honor ourselves and dishonor others as much as we can.

The fifth commandment of the ten given to Israel (and to us) is given with a blessing attached—a commandment to honor. Also, it's interesting to note that the first passage in the

Bible addressed to children is this one: "Honor your father and your mother [that's the command part], so that you may live long in the land the LORD your God is giving you [that's the blessing part]" (Exodus 20:12 NIV, additions mine). With that promise, God was impressing upon all of us the importance and benefit of honoring our parents and urging us to obey this commandment willingly. I guess God understood that if we struggled with honoring the authority of our parents, whom we live with and can see, it would be a greater struggle to honor other authorities that come into our lives (spouses, bosses, policemen, judges, and so on). Worse, it would be an impossible struggle to honor the authority of God, whom we can't see.

In all our homes growing up and raising children ourselves, honor has always had a preeminent place in everything we do. From a very early age we were taught to honor others. We taught our children that what we said was meant to be obeyed. *Honor was equated with obedience.* In fact, we determined when honor was enforced when our children were little, it would always return in a positive way when the child was older or grown. In our experience, teaching and enforcing honor resulted in a minimal level of rebellion in our children. Funny how that works. But rebellion will ultimately not produce happiness or peace, while honor will always produce happiness or blessing. Let's be honest. Rebellion against parents or other authority will never have a happy outcome. Therefore, rebellion against God not only doesn't have a happy outcome but, unchecked, will produce a very dire eternal consequence.

Let me give you a personal example of how this played out from my own childhood home.

"You have two weeks to break up with her."

I was eighteen years old and already in college and holding down a job, but I was still living in my parents' home in a Detroit suburb. My parents had been presented with an opportunity to go to Spain for two weeks through my father's workplace. They were excited and so were my siblings and I, because while they were gone, we would be overseen by an older lady from the church congregation who was a "softie," in our opinion.

The night before my parents were to leave town, my father called me into his bedroom. I assumed that since I was the oldest, he was going to somehow install me as second-in-command to watch over things—a responsibility I was only too willing to receive. Little did I realize what he was really going to ask of me. He didn't offer any preamble at all except to say, "Your mother and I have been talking, and I am going to ask you to do something for us by the time we get back home from Spain." He then went on to mess with my love life by declaring, "I want you to have your relationship with Mary broken off by the time we get back home." Notice he didn't say, "I would like," or "perhaps you would consider." Nothing of the sort. Just, "I want."

Well, I could hardly believe my ears. My mind began to race with every right reason why this request was beyond the scope of what he should be requesting at this stage of my maturity. And besides, how dare he! Didn't he realize that I thought I might love Mary? Did he not discern that she just might be "the one"? Did he not grasp the fact that I was already in college, had my own car, had my own job, was paying many of my own bills, and was almost independent (except when it came to eating three meals a day cooked by my mother, and my laundry always being done)? Did he not comprehend what this could do to my reputation among my peers?

This was the ultimate insult, the ultimate "ask," the ultimate control, and I wasn't going to go quietly or quickly—no, siree! Well, I let loose with all the above reasons and more. I didn't plead, I didn't try for compromise, I didn't negotiate. This was all-out war! If I were to lose the battle here, no telling how much independent ground I would ultimately lose. I was mad. I saw red. I even slapped the wall once, just to make my point. But it was no use. His mind wouldn't change. He just repeated, "You have two weeks to break up with her."

It wasn't that she wasn't a nice girl. She was. He admitted it. It wasn't that she was leading me down a wrong path. She wasn't. It wasn't that she came from a bad family environment. She didn't. And it wasn't that she was ugly. She wasn't. In fact, she had been in our home many times up to this point, and everyone seemed to like her and get along with her just fine, including, I might add, my parents. So where was this command coming from?

When questioned, all my father would say was, "We don't feel she's the one for you." Well, she felt right for me!

So, how was this resolved? By the time my parents returned home, I had broken off my relationship with Mary (although I do admit I dated her several more times during that two-week period and broke it off the night before they returned). Why did I succumb to such an unjustifiable request? Mainly because I had been taught from a very early age to honor my father and mother. I was taught that when I honor them and obey, things would ultimately go well for me and produce happiness and blessing. When I didn't, the opposite would always come to pass.

See, it was more important for me at eighteen years old to have my parents' blessing on my life than to run the risk of trying to create my own blessing. In other words, by teaching me and my siblings the principle of honor, we knew our parents loved us. We knew they knew things we didn't. And we knew they were responsible for making God's plan for our lives come to pass in our lives and for us to get on board with God's plan. So, when we submitted, in honor, to them (read: obey) it would always go well for us. We would live a long life!

In the long run, Mary wasn't the right one for me after all. My father has been right all along. After a few more brief relationships that didn't go very far, I soon met Susan, whom I married. On our wedding day, I was so glad I had taken my father's admonition to break it off with Mary. Mary found the right person for her, too, just as I found the right person for me. I'm so glad my father loved me enough to not be afraid of a headstrong eighteen-year-old son. And I'm so glad I honored him enough to listen and obey.

An Atmosphere of Honor . . .
- glorifies and praises God.
- respects parents, elders, and leaders.
- lifts people up rather than putting them down.
- sacrifices personal agendas for what God wants and others need.
- esteems, loves, and affirms others.
- recognizes that everyone has been created in the image of God.
- replaces arrogance with humility.
- equips servant leaders.

Creating an Atmosphere of Honor

In his book *Transformational Intelligence*, Dr. Joseph Umidi, one of my instructors at Regent University, points out that our real call in life is to *create culture*, not simply to worship culture or become a creature of culture. He goes on to state, "Every family, company, church, and community group is a candidate to model a creative approach to culture that maximizes the best in people and the potential of the culture to contribute to the uplifting of community and city. That maximization will require an intentional focus in our approach to transform the role of culture in our lives."[1]

Let me break that statement down for us and give a great example of how that might play out in your home. The type of culture Dr. Umidi is referring to here will be based in (1) healthy relationships, (2) with an intentional focus, (3) that maximize the best in each other.

Think of honor almost as a "gift" we are able to bestow on someone else. That "gift" of honor can transform every relationship, and that relationship can actually shift a culture. Honor is a relational or social term that identifies how people in any society evaluate one another. This is worked out in our homes. How we evaluate worth—ourselves, our siblings, our parents, and so on—affects our attitude and behavior toward others outside the home. Umidi further writes, "We need an upgrade of relational honor, a download of transformational behavior that will result in significance, productivity, loyalty, camaraderie, unity, identity, courage, and tenacity at home and work. In short, we need our home and work environments to become cultures of honor."[2]

Again, that's a lot to unpack, but let me clear it up a bit with this real-life example, particularly as it relates to the words loyalty, camaraderie, unity, and identity.

What do we mean by an *atmosphere of honor*? Honor begins with honoring God and extends to honoring others. God Himself teaches us this. He reveals in 1 Samuel 2:30 (NKJV), "for those who honor Me I will honor, and those who despise Me shall be lightly esteemed." And when it comes to honoring one another, we can turn to the apostle Paul's admonition in Romans 12:10, "Be kindly affectionate to one another with brotherly love, in *honor* giving preference to one another" (NKJV, emphasis mine).

When I read that verse of scripture, my mind always goes back to how my mother, Shirley, taught us kids the concept of honoring and preferring each other. If we ever had to share something—for example, a piece of toast—she set it up that whoever cut the slices had to let the other one choose which slice they wanted. In other words, we learned quickly never to short-change the other with a less than a 50/50 cut, but to get it as accurate as humanly possible. This made sure we were showing preference to the other. The apostle Paul would be happy.

Sarah Says

The main disciplinary issue we deal with in our home has to do with attitude . . . which is all about honor. When you have a bad attitude in the home, you are dishonoring your siblings (griping at them, yelling at them, smacking them, or trying to make their lives miserable in general). You are also going to eventually dishonor your parents with that bad attitude (talking back, disobeying, rolling your eyes when you thought they could not see). To us, a bad attitude is so important to deal with. A child who did not do a job you asked them to do may have been lazy, forgetful, or defiant. When we can determine that defiance was the problem, we deal with it more severely than if it was one of the other possibilities.

Defiance shows dishonor. As an adult, situations involving dishonor are going to cause more severe consequences and trouble than anything else. Dealing with those moments is very, very individual. We try to think creatively and individually about each child when it comes to discipline. For one, when they are young and middle-child ages, we typically remove them from the situation until they correct their attitude and can return respectfully. Sometimes, we all need a moment by ourselves to get our acts back together, right? We generally let the child come back on their own when they can have a better attitude with their siblings and parents. This works great in our house! If they come back and things have not changed, they return to their rooms and try again. Some children need more time than others. That is up to them. In our house, this starts as young as two and three years old. It may look a little different than with an older child, but it's really the same thing.

This atmosphere of honor includes thoughts, feelings, and actions that respect and lift others up while not seeking honor or glory for ourselves. This is so totally contrary to our current narcissism-fueled culture that the thought of instilling this principle can almost seem overwhelming to most parents. Let me encourage you, though. It's not impossible to display honor or demand it in the home. It's necessary. You just have to work very hard at keeping the culture outside the walls of your home from infiltrating the inside of your home. Think of yourself as a sentinel or a guard (the idea of a true guardian) for your home. You wouldn't let a robber or kidnapper inside without putting up a horrific fight in order to keep your children and family safe. Why wouldn't you respond the same with a culture that flows contrary to how you want your home to run and the way you want your children to turn out? Don't give in to a mindset that says, "Well, it's just the way kids act these days," or something similar.

When both of our kids were in their mid-teens—not quite adults and yet no longer children—there was always a lot of bickering going on between them. Our daughter was older, and our son wasn't happy about that. I'm sure my daughter had her way of somehow rubbing in that fact. Nonetheless, the fighting had finally gotten to the point that they couldn't even carry on a civil conversation with each other. Maddening. So, finally exhausted by it all, I called them into the living room one day along with their mother (who had plotted with me on how to deal with this situation). As they stood in front of me, I asked what the problem was, and, as typical in any home, both claimed in one long sentence "they didn't know" and "it was all the other's fault." Time for an honor lesson to build us some loyalty, camaraderie, and unity. Very simply, I told them both that from that day forward, until I saw a change in their attitude (read: looks, words, and actions) toward one another, they were no longer allowed to spend time with their friends. I informed them, to their shock and awe, that until they became each other's best friend, they weren't free to have any other friends. I thought they both were going to puke on my carpet. But we stood our ground, and lo and behold, they finally turned their relationship around. Today, they are best friends in their adult lives. Sometimes you must force honor, but it always pays off in the long run. For me, it paid off almost immediately, because I got the peace of my home back!

Shirley Says

A primary foundation of honor is obedience. The by-product of obedience, and immediate obedience, develops honor and respect of authority. No matter how you approach it as a parent, you are the first authority that child will ever know. You won't be the last! The teacher, the policeman, the sergeant in the army, the boss on the job will all evaluate the job you've done as a parent, based on that child's ability to conform to authority.

When they are two years old and you tell them to "come here," the way they are conditioned to respond to your command will determine their success in life. If you say "come here" and you end up chasing them, you have failed in teaching them obedience. You don't even allow your dog to get away with that!

If obedience hasn't been taught early on, then when you say "come" years later when they're about to run into the street or into a problem, they will ignore your voice, disobey the order, and suffer great consequence. No one wants that for their child.

What Dishonor Looks Like

As mentioned earlier in this chapter, the first law in the Bible addressed to children is to honor their father and mother.

Because all children are born in sin and rebellion (just to prove it, tell me what your child's first word was and I can almost guarantee it was the word NO!), it is also the first law they will try to break!

Dishonor will manifest itself in their life by three different means: looks, words, and actions. Each of these must be dealt with the very first time it occurs and must continue while that child is in our home, no matter the age. If not done consistently, the grown child, upon leaving the home, will not only remain immature the rest of their life but will struggle mightily with authority. They will always be known as people who are, at a minimum, hard to get along with and, at a maximum, always angry, irritable, and mean.

You know how those three words—looks, words, and actions—play out in your home without our explaining them to you. But just in case, let's review. "Looks" in a small child can often include a dramatic rolling of the eyes, not looking at you when you're talking to them or instructing them, or trying to give you their "mean" look. In an older child or teenager, it can manifest as a look of indifference or of listening to you with their ears and not their heart. If you're talking to them and they're still working on a text on their phone, get a clue. They are not listening to you. At times, it can even be a bit funny, but it still needs to be corrected immediately. Honor demands it. "Words" can be just the way something is said. It's not hard to determine if honor is missing in tone and inflection, and usually making your child restate something in the correct way will fix it. But sometimes "words" can even be abusive or hateful speech. We've all heard the child that tells the parent, "I hate you." If we ever thought to use that kind of speech or cop that kind of attitude with our mother, we would not only be recipients of serious attention (and read into that what you will) but also be pretty certain to receive even more attention when my father arrived home (and read into that what you will). You get my point.

Then there are "actions"—temper tantrums, the stomping of feet, hitting, breaking things, biting, and so on. All things that must be dealt with immediately and swiftly. Don't compromise in this area. Where do you think road-rage incidents begin? On the I-95 one day because so-and-so cut so-and-so off? Not! It began when at least one of those participants was allowed to slam something down in anger against authority, or even another sibling, and was never corrected and, therefore, got away with it. Honor was not maintained early in life, so why would anyone expect honor to be exhibited later in adulthood?

Sarah Says

Teenagers. As our kids have become teenagers, we have seen the need for a different type of correction. Teenagers often love to be in their rooms for long periods of time. By this age, it is no longer a negative experience, but is something they desire. Especially if they are having a day when emotions are rough and bad attitudes come easily. So in those cases, we look at the child and what is important to them. Do they have an attitude with the job they are doing? We will add another job that can be done when the first is completed well. If that is also done with a bad attitude, another job will come after. There are never shortages of jobs in our house!

But it is rare for a child to get more than two in a row. They figure that out real fast. For one of our children, taking away time with friends for the rest of that day makes a huge statement. For another, taking away electronic time has the biggest impact. And for another, their bad attitude almost always has to do with the amount of sleep they get, so an early bedtime is in order for that night. Which, I might add, seems like I was pulling their fingernails out with pliers for this particular child. Tell me to go to bed early one day. I'd love it!

Overall, we would much rather our kids learn how to control their bad attitudes and practice honor when they're just having a bad day or don't agree with someone else while they are still living in our home. The consequences here can make an impact, but are much easier lessons to learn now, rather than later in life. We have all met adults who have never learned to control their bad attitudes or honor those they are working with.

When you can learn to honor the people closest to you, the ones you see every day, the ones who can irritate you the most, like your siblings, it is a huge life lesson that will serve you well in whatever you pursue in life.

Isn't it interesting that when a parent tells a child to "come" and ends up having to count (1,2,3, . . .), that child seems to have an innate ability to know when to finally respond. When the response is never immediate and always flouts the authority over them, that is blatant dishonor.

Honor assumes "you want the best for me." That is best learned by consistent, loving, and immediate obedience.

There are many means of correcting and disciplining honor into children of all ages, and it usually requires a creative approach. The goal with any of these fixes or corrections is to make the situation too uncomfortable for the child to live with. It's called consequence. One such creative way is temporary isolation—"Leave until you can come back with a different look. Change your look!" By the way, just a thought here, but maybe tell the child to leave the dinner table until the attitude changes. When they feel it has changed, they can return. This might be just the thing you need to do to help them understand the importance you place on honor.

From the beginning, you want to put into a child the ability to trust *and* obey you. And really, that's the exact same thing God wants from us. He lovingly and creatively corrects us and does not leave us alone until we come to the point in our relationship that we can trust and obey Him, knowing that in doing so, it's going to go well for us.

A Final Takeaway of Common Sense

It has always helped me to think in terms of the bigger picture when it comes to this principle of honor and commonsense parenting. I remember that my father was intent on producing leaders in his children, not followers. I carried on that same tradition with my children. Leaders who honor God and others are often called "servant-leaders." This term is now being widely used by corporations in their leadership structures. These types of leaders embody the mandate of Galatians 5:13 (NKJV), "through love serve one another." One who honors others esteems the dignity, worth, and value of others without expecting some return for self. Honoring our parents refers not just to our biological parents but also to those surrogate parents that come into each of our lives, like teachers, leaders, bosses, mentors, coaches, and pastors who teach us by word and deed what is right, civil, kind, and polite. By the way, it might be good to stop right here and take an inventory of your relationship with your spouse, if you are married and raising children. Ask yourself, is honor being compromised by your words and actions toward each other? Or are your children hearing more compliments in the home than corrective or unflattering statements?

Sarah Says

One thing we look for as parents are opportunities that make a big impact. God-moments, so to speak, that allow the lessons we are trying to teach to *really* sink in. One day one of our teenagers, who normally does not deal much with attitude and dishonor, was going through a hard season. Hormones were kicking in, I imagine, and suddenly disrespect was becoming an issue. A small issue, for sure, but one we were not used to seeing from this child at all. That week, I was leaving for a cousin's wedding in St. Louis and taking our older kids with us, leaving Solo home with the younger kids. He had some work to do from home and was happy to let me go on without him. I was excited because I had previously lived in St. Louis as a child and love the city. Plus, I love all opportunities to spend time with my extended family. Because of my excitement, our older ones were also very, very excited about this short road trip. We pulled out of the driveway and were heading down our street when this same child, who had been struggling with a bad attitude for the last week or two with us and had also been picking fights with a particular sibling, all of a sudden had a very sassy, disrespectful sentence come out of his mouth. I looked at my mom, who was driving with us, and told her offhandedly that I was tempted to take this child back home and leave said child with Solo. She said, "Well, you know you could." I don't think it had actually occurred to me that I could! But her confidence gave me the courage to do it.

I silently turned that car around, went back to our driveway, and told my child to get his bag out of the trunk. I was met with much weeping and repenting, but I knew at the time that it was a God-opportunity to make a large impact on an attitude of disrespect that had been growing. I accepted his apology, but told him that this was necessary for him to really learn the lesson we were trying to teach him. I ran in and had a quick talk with my husband, who agreed immediately that it was the right thing to do. And I left my child there with his dad and all the little kids. He and his dad ended up having a good time together—lots of quality time, good talks, and they even found some fun. He was a changed child after that. He knew we were serious about dealing with his attitude. I wondered if he would be bitter about the missed experience, but he was not. This happened many years ago, and he has never again had an ongoing attitude problem like he did those few weeks. If he is struggling for a day or so, he now corrects it so fast. Since that time, Solo and I always look for those moments that God is giving us that are significant in the child's life and can make great impact. Not to deprive them of something just to deprive them, but rather to help them learn something faster and more permanently. We have seen providence put many such moments before us. Sometimes we are brave and use them, and a few times we have given in and not used them. No perfect parents over here! But the good news is, we always have another day to try again. Which is the message we are also teaching our children.

Branch Rickey, the great baseball player and sports executive known for having broken the color barrier in Major League Baseball by hiring Jackie Robinson to the Brooklyn Dodgers minor league team in 1945, is quoted as saying, "It is not the honor you take with you, but the heritage you leave behind." That's a big-picture statement. That's seeing down the road beyond just your children and into your grandchildren and great-grandchildren, should you live that long. Those words speak volumes to the character and virtue of honor that needs to mark the relationship between parent and child.

At thirty-seven, my son, Luke, was a managing director of a major US airline, overseeing approximately nine hundred customer-service employees at one of the airline's hubs. He started working for this airline part-time as an eighteen-year-old student, tossing bags underneath the plane, and had worked with them almost twenty years, moving up in the ranks as a young man until his next step, should he be fortunate, would be to become a vice president. He was often asked by his bosses how he could oversee men and women twice and sometimes three times his age and earn their respect as their boss. He always told his employers it was because he was raised in his father's (a pastor's) home and in church. He learned early on how to honor his sister and others! He learned how our leadership team at church honored one another, and how I endeavored to honor every single member of the church, no matter their age, gender, race, or ethnicity. He learned by observing, then instilling it in his own leadership and seeing the atmosphere of honor it produced.

Remember, what goes around comes around! As you instill in your children this principle of honor, it will come back not only to you but to your legacy and heritage of family well beyond your lifetime.

Commonsense Applications
- How has dishonor shown up in your home and how are you currently dealing with it?
- What ideas have you found that deal with dishonor effectively?
- Make a commitment to find ways to honor one another in your home. If there are two parents in the home, then make a commitment and plan to do this together. All spouses argue—that's a given—but inventory what your children might be hearing when you argue in front of them. Is honor being compromised by your words and actions toward each other? Or is your family hearing more compliments in the home rather than corrective or unflattering statements?

As a father, my purpose is not to pass on my seed, but to pass on my values.

—Dennis Prager

CHAPTER THREE

"Others May; You Cannot"

The Importance of Values

Defining Values

Others may, you cannot! Long before social media venues like Facebook, Twitter, and Instagram, we had a neighborhood communication system in place that was just as fast as today's internet advantages, and probably more complete and timely, to carry out the latest news happening in my childhood neighborhood in Detroit. Somehow, a word on anything always spread quickly, mouth to ear.

Much like today's social media connectivity, knowing what was happening in our friends' and neighbors' lives was just as important to us back in the fifties, sixties, and seventies. Particularly the important things like who got to do what, who got to go where, and who was currently enjoying the latest fad. Upon bringing the local news to the dinner table for consideration of these advantages currently being enjoyed and incorporated in other homes, we could typically count on my father to exclaim, "If you want that, then you can move in with them. However, we don't do that in this house." Talk about letting the wind out of our sails. My dad, at times, could be a complete "killjoy." My mother was even more to the point: "Others may. You cannot."

Sarah Says

My parents always told my brother and me, "We are Davids" whenever we complained about what the other kids were allowed to do, and we were not.

Ultimately, the fact that I didn't always wear the same "cool" clothes or go to the same "cool" parties or have the same "cool" experiences that some of my peers had, all worked to establish core values in my own life. Ultimately our values with regard to financial priorities, family time, and learning to be content, remove the need to be considered hip or "cool."

Through the leading of my parents, I learned that it's really okay to be different. I also learned how to resist peer pressure and cultural norms.

Let me tell you, you don't have eleven children in America today if you're afraid of what society thinks of you!

Not until I had my own home and was raising my own children did I begin to realize the importance of what my father and mother were doing when making and enforcing such statements. They were helping set and define the values that would govern our home and, more importantly, our behavior. That's exactly what values do. They govern us!

R. P. Lebret says it this way: "Civilization ceases when we no longer respect and no longer put into their correct places the fundamental values, such as work, family and country; such as the individual, honor and religion."[1] In other words, values shape not only you or your home but also the way a nation lives and prospers. Values are really nothing more than commonly held attitudes, beliefs, and characteristics which establish the core of what is important to us. John Adams wrote in 1798, "We have no government armed with power capable of contending with human passions unbridled by morality and religion [read: values] . . . Our Constitution was made only for a religious and moral people. It is wholly inadequate for the government of any other."[2] Fast-forward 224 years and it seems that the founding fathers' worst fears have been realized.

In my neighborhood, growing up among the many homes and families represented, whether they were identified or not, each family had its own set of values. My parents were determined to not only instill values in us but also instill *our* values. Some of these they learned from previous generations, some they established in their home for the first time, but each one could be identified, and none were committed to the circumstances or current "climate" (political, religious, economic, and so on) that seemed to always be telling us to change and conform. Thanks to both my parents, they didn't!

We may not realize it fully because we don't get up each morning thinking specifically about values, but they do influence our behavior and mission in life. They not only determine what is done but also how we go about getting things done. Our values, then, become the foundation for determining what is most important.

One of my friends reminded me recently of the story of the Empire State Building and other large buildings in the skylines of our major cities. It's amazing to look at them and realize that before any of those gigantic buildings came into physical existence, they first existed as a thought that, when shared with an architect, became a blueprint. Then, when contracted with a construction company, the plans became a reality when a foundation was laid, upon which the building was constructed.

The foundation of the Empire State Building in New York City was started in 1929. The building is constructed in such a way that it sways some five feet at the top and has been doing so since its completion in December 1931. Can you imagine the amount of pressure that is applied to that foundation?

Without a solid, well-constructed foundation, the building would not last. The foundation holds and stabilizes the entire structure, including the elemental pressures applied to it by the force of nature.

In a similar sense, the foundation we instill into our children is the most important part of their development. That foundation holds and stabilizes their entire life, even during the times of greatest change, uncertainty, and pressure. When there are no values to support, guide, or provide the basis for decision making, their life, and subsequently the lives of their children (the subsequent generations), will not stand against the pressures exerted against them. And you can be sure (think of your own life), pressure will come! It's a certainty.

The apostle Paul recognized this important principle of values when he cautioned a whole generation to be careful how they built their lives and their churches on the previous generation's work. We can apply his instructions to our lives and homes today. It's such good wisdom.

Using the gift God gave me as a good architect, I designed blueprints; [others are] putting up the walls. Let each carpenter who comes on the job take care to build on the [correct] foundation! Remember, there is only one foundation, the one already laid: Jesus Christ. Take particular care in picking out your building materials. Eventually there is going to be an inspection. If you use cheap or inferior materials, you'll be found out. The inspection will be thorough and rigorous. You won't get by with a thing. If your work passes inspection, fine; if it doesn't, your part of the building will be torn out and started over. . . . Don't fool yourself. Don't think you can be wise merely by being [up-to-date with the times]. . . . **What the world often calls smart, God calls stupid.**
(1 Corinthians 3:10–15, 18–19)

That's some serious and accurate advice, no matter what your religious background might be. The same principles work in church, business, and education, but most certainly in building our families. And when Paul talks about an inspection that makes things much more serious. I don't like inspections, and most people don't. If I try to gloss things over and make it all "appear" to be in order, a good and thorough inspection will uncover my attempt at faking it. I read a quote once that said, "You never really know how well you have raised your children until you see how your grandchildren turn out." When I first read that as a young father, it blew my mind. The idea made sense, but the task of raising my own two children became a much greater and sober endeavor. Now I had to start thinking long-term, beyond just raising my two for eighteen to twenty years and then getting them out of the house and on their way. I had to think in terms of what values their mother and I wanted to instill in them that would stand up to any inspection and any outside pressure.

Shirley Says

This chapter on values is so very important, but what is more important is that prior to beginning your parenting role—particularly if you are a dual parent home—to be well grounded in your own values first. (And if there are two parents, you need to be in agreement with your values, prior to parenting.) If you are in agreement, it will make your job so much easier as a parent. If both mother and father are on the same page, it will always be harder for your children (who are gifted at manipulation from birth) to figure out how to separate you by getting you as parents to contradict each other. Children quickly figure out which parent is the pushover and which is the hard-nose. Which one says yes more easily, and which one says no first. However, when you are firm in your values, then you will present a unified and uncompromising front. Those values then govern the home and the children in that home. They will realize your values can't and won't bend to the moment. Those values not only guide and protect them in the home but also protect them when they're outside of the home, and it teaches them the importance of values for later use when they have their own family. For example, when we were raising our children, we taught them to respect others' property and space. They learned to knock on our door before entering. In the same way, we balanced that value with the understanding that we kept no secrets. They knew at any moment they could be required to give an account of their actions or have their sock drawer inspected. It was our own version of "trust, but verify." Values are nothing if they're not enforced and lived out. Our children knew early on what was considered contraband, and an inspection could occur any moment without advanced warning. Those values were important to us and were instrumental in their character formation.

My advice when it comes to values is that you must have a vision as to what you want your children to become in character and integrity. As I stated earlier, you have to know your personal values prior to parenting. Then once those values are established, refuse to compromise, no matter how much pressure you receive from any source, including your children, your extended family, or the society in which you live. Establish the needed values ahead of actually parenting (whether you learned them in your own childhood home or add them to your adult home), then refuse to compromise no matter how much your child begs you or society condemns you as being out of touch or judging you as too strict and unbendable. They're not the ones responsible for your children; you are! You want your children to contribute to society in a positive and honoring way, and that goal begins with your values. Remember: "Others may. You may not."

We start with values because most strategic parenting fails when values are not articulated early enough in the process. If core values are not established, the clear direction we seek to enjoy as parents is also difficult to establish. Ultimately, we prioritize our time, energy, focus, and money according to our values. It is wise to clarify your personal values, or the core values you want in your home, and then make sure you prioritize your time, money, and parenting to live out those values. If you are unclear about what your core values are, or unfamiliar with how to formulate some, then it's our hope that this section will greatly benefit you.

What worked for me in confronting this great responsibility was to create in my mind's eye a vision of what I wanted my children and grandchildren to look like. I knew they'd all be good-looking physically, because their mother and grandmother are so good-looking! But this "look" was different. This had to do with how they would look and live in behavior and attitude. And that's when I began to reflect on the values I had been taught by and received from my parents that were probably passed down from generations before them. I made a list of things I felt were the most important to us and our family. Now, your list will probably be different, as well it should be. Your list might also include some values and attributes from my list. Whatever the case, I hope this gets each of us thinking a bit more deeply, and certainly more long-term, when it comes to raising children.

Sarah Says

As most of you may know, I married a man from a very different culture from the other side of the world.

We had vastly different upbringings, family dynamics, cultures. We certainly had different personalities and even different goals in life.

I wanted to live somewhere in Africa, but he wanted to live anywhere in the world. He wanted to pastor, but I wanted to do anything *but* pastor. I wanted anywhere from four to twelve children, and he graciously agreed to three or four.

Even with all those differences, we had almost identical values when it came to our beliefs, our convictions, and the general way we wanted to live our lives. For example, we each wanted to live a generous life serving others. We each were determined to only serve where we felt God was leading us. We even had similar work values.

Because of these basic core values, we haven't experienced huge conflicts in our marriage or in raising children. We almost always find ourselves on the same page regarding our decisions about life and parenting. And when we don't, it's not hard to find a place of compromise, because we share the basic core values.

By the way, that doesn't mean we don't have a real good and loud argument on occasion!

Values Matter

Values are the ideals, standards, and core beliefs we are passionate about. These values communicate what's important to us. They are our primary or core beliefs. A belief is a conviction or opinion we hold to be true. Values are nonnegotiable and must be lived out in daily practice. When articulated and lived out consistently, values are what keep us on track. Communicating values must precede moving forward with vision, because vision (for our own lives and the lives of our children and grandchildren) is built on the foundation of our values. Values are the glue that bonds family to each other even into successive generations.

Roy Disney (Walt's brother) said it this way: "It's not hard to make decisions, once you know what your values are."[3] Values, or core principles in our lives, guide us, guard us, and govern us. They are unceasing, fervent convictions that bring clarity to our thoughts and actions. Let me see if I can't break this down better for you.

- **Core values are perpetual.** Core values change very slowly. This is why marriage can be so difficult. It's the blending of two sets of values. If those values are opposing opposites, then conflict is going to happen. (On a side note here, that is what an engagement period is all about! Not if you're compatible in bed or sexually, but if you are compatible in your value systems. You'll save yourself a lot of grief if you explore this area *first* and *before* the relationship advances too far. It takes a substantial length of time to change individual values, and even longer when you're dealing with a group. Consequently, it's critical to begin with the right standards.)

- **Core values are enthusiastic.** *Vision* is a seeing word; *enthusiasm* is a feeling word. Core values are heartfelt and elicit strong emotions. They stir feelings that can move people to live rightly or wrongly. They can elevate or devalue the individual. They go beyond any political or social stance someone might hold, and they eventually determine how a family member operates and treats other members of the family—even how a nation will treat its own citizens.

- **Core values are based in Scripture.** I chose to include this point because it certainly is true concerning our family's core values. It may or may not be the case for you. However, you should realize you're going to pick up core values from somewhere. The David family chooses to base our values on Scripture, and we feel strongly that Scripture is the ultimate truth that gives us the values we choose to incorporate into our lives. The true test of an intrinsic values statement comes from asking yourself, "What are my values rooted in?" Without sounding preachy, I do believe that while your values may not necessarily be found in the Bible, they should be rooted in scriptural principles.

- **Values are core convictions.** A conviction is a deep-seated opinion or belief you hold to be true based on limited evidence.

- **Values guide, guard, and govern our lives.** Values are deeply ingrained convictions that inform and direct how decisions are made, money is spent, risks are taken, problems are solved, goals are set, and priorities are determined. This is true for every one of us, every one of our families, any good organization, and even any country.

Therefore, the quality and strength of the foundations we lay and hold to in our lives will determine the heights reached by us in living out our lives. This truth becomes even more important for your children and grandchildren. Values (or another great word—virtue) by itself is no guarantee of right action, which requires more than good intentions. In addition, we need both wisdom to know what the right thing to do is and the will to do it.

Our Values

We thought long and hard before beginning this portion of this chapter. Our hesitation came from not wanting to appear haughty or snobbish. Neither did we want to, in any way, subject the reader to our core values with an underlying thought that our values are the ones you should be incorporating into your family. Nothing could be further from the truth. The values we list here may or may not be on your list. We would love to have the ability to talk and share about what values matter to each of you. That would be such an interesting conversation and would certainly be a way we could learn a lot more about each other and learn from each other. With that in mind, these are listed in no particular order.

- **Loyalty.** Our loyalties are important symbols of the kind of persons we have chosen to become. They indicate a steadfastness in our attachments to those other persons, groups, institutions, or ideals with which we have deliberately decided to associate ourselves and our names. Learning to be a loyal friend or worker began for us in the home with our siblings.

- **Giving.** This value makes sure there is a generous spirit instilled in each of the children we're raising. Children, by nature, are selfish. Children that never have that selfishness confronted, end up being selfish and self-centered adults. They love only themselves and have very little use for others except what they can get out of them. Typically, a child's first word they learn after the word *no* is the word *mine*. Now, it's not bad for each to have their own things, but that's different from being selfish. A generous spirit goes a long way from thinking what we have is ours. We are blessed by God in various measures, and God Himself set this pattern of giving by giving the world His Son, Jesus Christ. A generous spirit instills the value of loving others even more than yourself.

- **Truthfulness and Honesty.** I can never think of this value without looking around for the "little bird." Let me explain.

My mother always told us that a little bird would tell her when we were lying. I never could find that little bird, no matter how hard I tried. But once I became a parent, I realized that God gifts us as parents with an ability to discern when a child is lying to us. Whether it's a shuffling of the feet or an inability to look us in the eye, we know when we're being buffaloed. Honestly, this is not an easy value to instill. We all have that lying nature hardwired into us since Adam and Eve got caught eating the forbidden fruit! When the lie didn't work, Adam quickly blamed Eve for the fall. What a guy! As a parent, I came to realize why this value is so important to our character. If we get away with telling a lie to others and become comfortable with lying, we will soon get comfortable with telling ourselves lies. If you start doing that, there will be absolutely no good that comes from it. That's the most destructive thing we can do to ourselves!

- **Gratitude.** This value continues to address selfishness, just as giving does. But while giving instills a generosity into the character of a child, gratitude instills an appreciativeness for the little things. This value doesn't come naturally to most of us. When Grandma, on a fixed and limited income, sends a single dollar bill in a card for that child's birthday, they should be just as grateful as they would be for that rich uncle sending a one hundred-dollar bill. Instilling this value makes us value others as equals. It helps remove prejudice and its effects. Most importantly, gratitude has the ability to remove competitiveness (the wrong kind) out of us. To have the ability to be grateful in all types of circumstances serves us well in later life. Start by teaching your child to say thank you every time they receive something. That way they won't assume that life, or somebody, "owes" them anything.

Sarah Says

One practical way you can instill the values into your children is when you actually show them. Action speaks louder than words.

For example, when you find an opportunity to give, bring your children in on that adventure so they see the value being executed and the results that come from that value. When you find an opportunity to serve in an area that needs help, before you go and do it, consider bringing a child or the whole family along with you. They will have their eyes opened to the world around them, they will get to share in the warm feelings of a need met, and they will begin to form your values into their own world. It's a sermon without preaching!

Let me give you a real-life example. A value that Solo and I share is recognizing the sovereign hand of God in our lives. We went through a season where we had very little money. And at one point, I remember we had a list of needed groceries with no money to purchase them. One day when things started feeling a bit stressed and desperate, we came home after being out on an errand and found *all* the groceries on our list, plus more I would have bought given the ability, sitting at our front door in several boxes. To this day, we still don't know who it was that supplied all these goodies, because we had told no one about these needs.

You can imagine how wonderful a blessing this was. We called the kids into the kitchen, showed them what had happened, and told them how great a value believing that God is watching over us actually is. We prayed and thanked God as a family. We even took pictures!

Understand this: we planted in our children that day, by this experience, a core value they will never forget.

They not only learned a little better how to trust God but also learned how wonderful the values of generosity, giving, serving, and disciplined living are.

What a lesson. And they still remember that day to this day!

- **Disciplined Living.** Susan and I determined early on that we did not want our children living in our basement when they were thirty! My father and mother felt the same way about us three boys. Can you blame them? Each one of us had to live by a schedule of sorts once we were out of diapers. You got up in the morning at a certain time, you practiced your musical instrument (Mother set the timer), you did your homework (and they checked), you completed your assigned chores (and they checked), and if you had a job, you went and did it! On top of that there was school, sports, church, and a multitude of other activities that took up our time. What there was no time for was laziness or lying around. When you said you were going to do something or be somewhere, you were disciplined to that. And according to my father, if you're five minutes early, you're on time, if you're on time, you're late, and if you're late, don't bother!

- **Serving.** Maybe at this point you're starting to see a pattern shaping up in the values that were instilled in us. Almost all of these values are designed to help children see beyond themselves. Serving also contributes greatly to that attribute. In a culture that seems to pride itself in "looking out for number one," serving challenges that very notion. Philippians 2:3–8 provides the perfect guide. Here is my paraphrase of these verses. "God, teach our children to humbly consider others better than themselves. May they look not only to their own interests but also to the interests of others." Again, that confronts that selfish nature that's in each of us. This value was modeled to us over and over again in our home. My father worked two jobs for most of my childhood, yet he was the greatest of servants to my mother and us children. My mother self-lessly served her husband and us in countless ways, and we also were taught to serve the home, or the neighbors, or at church, as expected. I can remember, as a teen with a lot of things on my plate and a busy schedule both academically and socially, when our elderly neighbor's wife, Mrs. Gilbert, suffered a massive stroke. She spent several years in a wheelchair in a small part of their home, while her husband served his wife and took care of her completely. However, one day, my father noticed Mr. Gilbert beginning to tire and wear down. He offered him my services to come over often to sit with Mrs. Gilbert and keep her company and watch for anything unusual, just so Mr. Gilbert could get out and get a break every once in a while. My presence sure blessed him, and it taught me to look around and find ways to serve others with anything I had, including my time.

- **Respect.** Again, this confronts that selfishness in us. Oh, how we enjoy receiving respect and will make a very big deal of things if we feel we are being slighted or maligned in any way. We're quick to stand up for ourselves but not so quick to give others respect or support. We were taught very early to respect our elders, respect those in authority (that is, teachers, principals, pastors, and so on), to respect women, and generally respect all men everywhere. We were taught to talk only when spoken to and not interrupt, and to keep our opinions and thoughts to ourselves until we were asked for them. I'm told we have a race problem in our country right now, but it hasn't shown up in our home and proba-bly won't. We were taught, and continue to teach the next generation, to respect everyone they encounter, whatever the skin color, whatever the economic status, and whatever the status or station in life. This value needs to make a return into our homes, our communities, and our culture.

Well, that's quite a list we have, but each one of those values shaped us as children and now serve us as adults. I realize my parents could have set up a whole system of rules and do's and don'ts and other guidelines and action items in our lives. They did a little, of course, but mostly they just kept reinforcing our family values. They didn't get much blowback from any of us for trying to immerse ourselves in the culture of our day. (And this was during the crazy time of hippies, free sex, and drugs designed to "blow your mind.") They didn't set rules about dress, hair length, or curfews. I think they realized they couldn't possibly address all of the possible pitfalls. Instead, they just kept reinforcing the core values. They knew core values affect everything.

That reminds me of a little story to share with you in closing out this chapter. It is rumored that upon the death of President Franklin Roosevelt, near the end of World War II, Sam Rayburn, Speaker of the House of Representatives, took Vice President Harry Truman aside and said to him, "You're going to have a lot of people around you telling you what a great man you are, Harry. But you and I both know you ain't."

Sam Rayburn was judging Truman by his low-key and non-charismatic personality. In Rayburn's mind, Truman didn't have much to offer or bring to the table at this important juncture in American history. Roosevelt was such an overwhelming force of personality that Truman was mostly overlooked and underrated by the political elite. However, Truman ended up being a very good president because his core values were fundamentally strong, and they guided all his decisions during his presidency.

Core values are everything. So . . . what values are you passing on? Remember how we started this chapter and how you can now apply core values into your home: *Others may, you cannot.*

Commonsense Applications

- Think about what core values are nonnegotiable in your family. Then, make a list of the five or six core values. If they are not present currently in your family, write a brief plan of action to begin incorporating those values into your home. Don't worry if you think it's too late! It's never too late to begin something this important. Commit to implementing these values tomorrow, then track your progress.

Suffer the pain of discipline, or suffer the pain of regret.
—Unknown

CHAPTER FOUR

"Let the Punishment Fit the Crime"

The Principle of Discipline

The Art of Creative Discipline

"Let the punishment fit the crime" was the go-to foundation of parenting for my parents, for Susan and I, and even now for our children. By parenting with this mantra, you become the most creative in your parenting years, because you do not either (1) ignore bad behavior or (2) revert to a default response every time discipline is required. For example, screaming, hitting, or exploding in anger hardly ever do anything to bring about correction or maturity. These reactions as a parent actually produce fear or resentment, and only produce a momentary emotional relief for the screamer. When that happens, the sad result is that those responses are usually employed by successive generations, with the same results.

When I contemplate my childhood, I believe my mother excelled the most with her ability to be creative at discipline. She would determine what each infraction was composed of, then devise a corresponding punishment that brought about the needed discipline or training. The best part? She never used the same punishment twice in a row.

For example, lying and rebellion were much more serious in her mind because those areas involved our character. In her mind, these were high crimes and misdemeanors against the state. Like any good state prosecutor, she would pursue these infractions with considered analysis and deliberation. Once it was determined that serious defects of character had occurred, she then moved quickly through presenting her case. On rare occasions we would be allowed to briefly defend ourselves. And just like any good criminal attorney will tell you, you should never defend yourself, but keep your mouth closed and hire a good attorney. Needless to say, there was very rarely anyone capable or willing to defend us. My two brothers sure weren't inclined to take my case. Besides, we were no match for the greatest prosecutor within an eight-block perimeter around Hillcrest Street in Detroit.

"Alright, mister," she would start. "You lied to me" or "You totally disobeyed my explicit orders." And that was the sum total of her closing arguments. With that, she rested her case. Verdict equals guilty. Then with one quick breath, we would move immediately into the sentencing phase. Oh, we always tried an appeal. Hardly ever worked. In fact, I have racked my memories and don't ever remember when an appeal did work. I remember using a mercy plea quite often. We appealed to her good character and nature. We appealed with promises to forgo our sinful life and walk the straight and narrow from that moment forward. We even tried bypassing her and appealing to the Sovereign God and His Son Jesus, asking for His forgiveness. Nothing mattered. We had upended the forces of nature, had tilted the earth off its axis, had offended the heavens with our infraction, and it required a penalty, a penance, a punishment. With bated breath we would stand for the passing of sentence. Depending on the crime, the punishment would be meted out. Very rarely was it something we had experienced before. My mother, with only a high school education, could come up with the most ingenious and creative punishments. Our current court systems could use her right now!

She saw each of these moments as teachable moments. First and foremost, they were each, in their own way, designed to teach us personal responsibility. Today, I watch some of these young adults tagging buildings with spray paint, or destroying someone else's property, or, worse, burning down buildings and people's businesses. They could use my mother.

Her rule of law extended beyond the four walls of our home. I remember one time my brother's best friend decided to soap our windows on Halloween when he knew we weren't going to be home. When we came home and found the windows soaped, my brother confessed that he knew it was his neighborhood friend. The very next day, when that young man came around, my mother had a sudsy bucket and brush ready for him. She made him and my brother both clean all the windows. My brother was made to help because it was his friend, and she considered it a good life lesson. Maybe she also thought it would take a bit of the sting out of making the friend do it alone. They did it, and in doing so, learned a valuable lesson. You don't mess with someone else's stuff, and if you do, you will make restitution.

That young man's mother, however, pitched a fit at my mother for this lesson. Their approach to teaching personal responsibility was evidently much different than my parents'. Their son was never allowed to play much with my brother after that. Last we heard, that young man had a hard time with life and addictions. Not sure where he is today. I can almost assume that if my brother had been the one doing the soaping, he would not only have been made to clean the neighbors' windows, he would have probably been sent to clean both sides of the entire block and not come home till the job was completed.

Again, punishment has to have a purpose. It should be designed to cause us to take responsibility for our actions which results in a disciplined life. My mother knew anyone can be sorry, even genuinely so. But a lesson is learned by discipline, and she was not afraid to apply it. As a parent, she knew she was not our friend. Rather, she was our authority until we left the house. She was determined to treat every moment as a teaching moment, both in a positive sense and a negative sense.

Shirley Says

I was often asked, "How does a mother with three young, boisterous boys keep them all in line when you're out and about?" Simple. If one of them became unruly while I was shopping, I made that one hang onto my skirt until they decided they would behave as they were taught. I found that drastically curtailing their freedom for a moment or so would quickly result in a more responsible, behaved response. The more you behaved, the more freedom you earned.

What was really fun was when I'd be shopping and all three boys were hanging onto my skirt. You can't believe the looks I got!

I hate lima beans. They have to be one of the nastiest vegetables ever put on earth by God. I'm not sure what He was thinking. The first time they were served on my dinner plate, just looking at them almost made me gag. Seriously. Just the look of those little green nuggets of sand triggered something in me, so I sat there and refused to even consider eating one. My parents took much of them away, but left a few on the plate and required me to finish them. They did offer certain temporary solutions like, "Eat them along with something else on your plate" or "Swallow them with a gulp of milk." But I wasn't going to do it. Now, at this point, I'm not sure my mother was concerned for my nutritional health (should there even be any nutritional value in a lima bean), but she was insistent I try something I may not like. Although I may not enjoy it, I would at least have tried and conquered my fear or my reflex action. Well, I refused. So we had a showdown. Once again, the creative side came out of my mother. "Eat what's on your plate or don't eat anything until the next meal."

Now, I know this sounds extreme to many of you reading this. But there was an important life lesson she was teaching me. There are always going to be things that I do like and don't like doing in life. That doesn't mean I can escape them. That doesn't mean I can just live for myself. I had to learn that day, that although I have certain likes and dislikes, life doesn't always allow me to take the one and leave the other. In fact, looking back over my career and the different jobs I have held, not once was any job without its usual downside. Most of the time I enjoyed the job, but each job also came with a task or two that I would do everything in my power to avoid. Eating those four or five lima beans that day taught me that sometimes I have to stuff the gag reflex, take a big gulp of milk, and get the distasteful job done. That lesson has served me well over the years.

Now, there were other much less severe breaches and trespasses that we engaged in growing up. My mother was no less consistent, even when it came to all sorts of matters both big and small. I remember a few occasions when two of us boys were fighting or arguing and she'd had her fill of such nonsense. She would issue each of us a paper and pen. We were told to go to the dining room table and write out what happened in our own words. Present our case, so to speak. That would be fine, but she then added a caveat that kept us from sinking into the mire of "he said, he said."

"Both your papers must agree," she decreed, "about what happened before you can consider the project complete. Then bring the papers to me and I'll decide."

Well, that totally took the air of smug superiority right out of us. Fact is, usually after completing the assignment, we would not even have any side left to call our own, and the problem was solved. Thinking back on it, I just had a huge regret! I should have used this same tactic in pastoring couples who had come into my office for marriage counseling. I should have installed a dining room table in my office. It would have saved me hours of listening to their gripes.

Sarah Says

Creative discipline takes a lot of energy on behalf of Mom and Dad! Often Solo and I will take a step back and talk together about a behavior we are seeing in our children that we need to be more creative with in our punishment and discipline. We probably do not have the gift of Grandma that can call out a creative punishment on the spot. But that's okay! We still find it eventually. Where there is a will, there is a way.

When children are fighting continuously, we make them work together on a project. They may need to weed the garden or clean the basement or organize the pantry. This technique has worked well for us. The children in question may continue their arguing for a while, but they eventually realize that the work will not come to an end until they learn to work *together.*

We have employed the same tactic for fighting in the car. In the past, we have often just separated the fighting children in question to different places in the van. However, some children do not let the boundaries of space get in the way of a good fight. In that case, we have learned the best thing is to actually have them sit together. Way in the back, so the rest of us do not have to suffer too much while they work through their differences. This solution is *not* their favorite thing when they are completely disgusted with that particular sibling on that particular day! But we have seen some great compromises and friendships come out of a road trip in which two kids learned that they actually could enjoy one another's company in close quarters. And they *do* eventually figure it out.

While fighting with each other or poking, pinching, pushing, prodding, and pulling were more nuisance crimes, my mother didn't ignore things. In fact, to our dismay, she was always consistent and thorough. Although once when a neighbor called her to tell her that two of her boys were out on the sidewalk fighting like mad, she asked the neighbor, "Can you see any blood?" The neighbor replied, "No, of course not." My mother's response? "Oh, that's good. I told them not to bring that stuff to me unless there's blood or someone's unconscious." The neighbor was mortified, but we never heard from her again on that subject.

The Traps We Fall Into

The thing I never heard either of my parents utter were numbers. Let me explain. Through the years, I have always been amazed that other kids could get their parents to count. You've heard them as well, I'm sure. You're standing in line at the check-out and a child (of any age) is giving the parent pure fits and not obeying a word the parent is uttering. The parent then makes the generic threat, "I'm going to count to three and if you don't stop that, young man, you're going to get it." Well, the young man already knows the breaking point for the parent. Sometimes it's the number three, and the minute that number is spoken, the child stops. More often than not, the child knows that the parent could count to a thousand and still nothing is going to happen. The threat is without teeth or follow-up, so why bother paying any attention to it? The score then becomes Parent 0 / Child 1.

I recall a comedian talking about this problem once. He said he'd tried this counting tactic on his mother once. When he was disobeying, before his mother could start counting, he said, "One." He told his audience he awoke from his coma four days later. I have a feeling that would have been the same in my household if I had tried that on either my father or my mother. There was never any compromise or negotiation given to obedience. You either obeyed immediately, or you were subject to a variety of punishments and penalties. I think that is how obedience is learned. Punishment must be immediate and consistent and correspond to the infraction. The sooner your child understands those parameters, the better off they will be.

As a parent, if I instruct my two-year-old to come here to me, they had better turn around and come. The worst fight I ever got into with my mother-in-law happened one day when my daughter Sarah was about eighteen months old. We were at my in-laws' home for dinner. As we got ready to leave, I held Sarah's coat, and she immediately turned and ran from me. I calmly called her name and told her to come. She turned to look at me, then immediately turned around and ran away from me again. My mother-in-law thought the rebellion was cute. I didn't. I quickly overtook Sarah, turned her around while telling her, "You need to come when I tell you to come," and I helped move her along with my hand sternly up against her swaddled bottom.

You would have thought I had just crucified my in-laws' only granddaughter. I was told how inhuman and cruel and unfeeling I was. I was reminded that she was still a small child under two years of age. In my mind, my mother-in-law inferred that I was not worthy of such a precious child, and I would surely find myself for all eternity hanging out in the lake of fire.

Shirley Says

One day when Jerry was about two years old, I decided to take him to the department store in downtown Detroit with me. J. L. Hudson's was huge and had multiple floors with both escalators and elevators. I had no idea that the escalator would terrify him. When it came time to go down a level, I took his hand in mine but, to my surprise, he froze, dug in his heels, and refused to budge. I swatted him once on his diapered behind and told him to step on now. He finally did.

He needed to learn to trust and obey, and the escalator presented a perfect teaching moment for that lesson. He ended up riding with me on the escalator, holding my hand, all the way down. Another lady also rode down with us . . . telling me what a terrible mother I was all the way. I just smiled at her, and thought how lucky my son was that I was his mother and not her.

My persistence taught Jerry a valuable lesson that day. From that moment on, he knew that escalators were not a bad thing, and he could enjoy riding them, which he did going forward. But he also learned that I was in charge and in command, and I knew what was best for him. I learned not to be intimidated by what other people thought of my approach to discipline.

He still likes escalators!

I knew from my own upbringing that obedience must be immediate and without question. As the parent, I have the best interest of that child in mind when I require obedience. I knew from my mother that one day I might find that child, when she's older, running toward the street or something and unable to see the oncoming car. My child needs to know my voice, know when I mean what I say, and turn around and obey.

Doing so just might save her life one day. There's no time in those circumstances to count to three, so why set that child up to respond only to escalating threats when it is much more vital they learn simple obedience? Try counting to three with a dog you're trying to train. It doesn't work. They will look at you like you're nuts.

The Benefit of Consistent Discipline

I've mentioned it already, but my mother's disciplining strategy required a total commitment to consistency. I don't recall there ever being a time when she let a needed discipline moment slip away or be ignored. I don't know where she found the energy, but she was relentless. Now, make no mistake, she didn't hound us or hover over us waiting for one of us to slip up. She didn't try to control our every waking moment. What she did was display a willingness to confront or investigate everything that needed investigation. In other words, she never told us "I'm too busy" by her words or her actions. She never said, "I don't have time for that" by her words or actions. To the contrary, she displayed a problem-solver attitude and, as we got older, taught us how to be problem-solvers.

I think I've figured out her secret. Besides being unwavering in her pursuit of justice and the American way (like Superman), she was the ultimate inquisitor. She would have been an excellent FBI agent. She knew how to ask probing questions and pursue any rabbit trail necessary to get to the bottom of any issue, fight, conflict, or lie. And she didn't jot down a single note. Everything was all contained and stored in her memory, which was formidable. You might, for example, try and shape a narrative (*lie* is such a harsh word, don't you think?), and she would remind you that six months ago, during a previous interrogation, you had actually said something totally different, to which she would respond, "Now, which is it?"

So her consistency was multifaceted. First and foremost, as I've mentioned, she was tireless. I actually think a child is smart enough to either try and wear a parent down and become just plain wearing to the parent (and I should know; I once was a child), or seek to find that parent at a low or exhausting moment and go in for the kill. It doesn't even have to be over a bad thing. If you can find Mom or Dad when they're distracted, tired, dazed, frustrated, or irritated, you usually have a better chance of getting away with something or getting the answer or permission you seek. Not so with my mother. Not even so with my father. They made a daunting team. I can't ever remember getting my dad to say yes to something that my mother had said no to. Their consistency in discipline approach was foolproof. The response we always got to that particular type of set-up of our parents was "What did your mother say?" with an immediate follow-up, "Then why did you come and bother me and ask me? Do you want trouble, young man?"

Notice, if you will, by their responses, that they were pretty consistent with their approach to us as well. They hardly ever made statements to us once we had achieved the age of account-ability (meaning responsible now for our own actions—in Jewish tradition, usually around thirteen years of age, and we're not even Jewish). They always used a question. That put the responsibility squarely back on us. In other words, my son, you are going to learn that your every action has a built-in, corre-sponding opposite and equal reaction for which you are respon-sible. I think we could use a whole bunch of that in our nation right now. Can I get an amen?

The second way they were consistent was they were always teaching, and always teaching us to an end goal. As I mentioned in chapter 3, we have to set a goal for our chil-dren. What do we want of them? What do we expect of them? What are our hopes and dreams for their future? That goal has to remain a consistent reminder and force in your life as a parent and it has to be applied, fairly, in every facet of your child's life. Pressures of life emanating from work, finances, conflicts, and sickness will drain you of energy physically, mentally, and emotionally. Consistency in parenting fights those pressures and sees the bigger picture of a long-term goal. The long-term goal in this case is planting trees and carving pillars—raising your children.

Sarah Says

Sometimes we have a situation with a child that needs to be corrected, and it is much bigger than a little fight with a sibling or a day of a rotten attitude. Once, one of our boys was consistently struggling to get schoolwork done. His attitude around school had truly turned rotten. He made working together with him on school subjects painful for both him and me, his teacher! Turning assignments in, learning new topics, and getting his work done day to day were all becoming a really big problem in our home. We were at a loss as to how to deal with our discipline issue with this child. I remember waking up one morning, though, with the exact right solution. I believe it was a thought straight from God because I do not think I could have come up with it myself. In fact, it sort of scared me to think about! But I presented the idea to Solo and he agreed immediately that it was the best thing to do. We were going to kick him out of school.

You might think it sounds crazy to kick a child out of homeschool. We actually would agree with you . . . it was crazy. But we sat our child down and told him that since he obviously did not appreciate school any longer, not only would he not have to do it, he would no longer even be *allowed* to do it. At first, of course, he was ecstatic. We were not surprised by this response. But days turned into weeks. His siblings were all doing school. He was not allowed to fill up any school time with electronics or socializing with neighbors, but could read or find quiet activities to do so he did not disturb the rest of the house as we went about our normal routine. This routine became pretty boring for him quickly. Beyond that, we had many conversations about future careers with all our children at the dinner tables during those weeks. Of course, we casually included in our conversations the education needed for such careers. We were well aware of this particular child's motivation with money. Turns out he wanted to be back in school! But we did not immediately let him return. We wanted to make sure there would be real change on his part. So, after a period of about six weeks, we finally let him return to his schoolwork. Since that point, he has been a completely different student who takes responsibility for his own work and is very diligent. This lesson took place six years ago, and we are still reaping its benefits to this day.

Their personal future success demands it, their future spouse demands it, their future boss or employees demand it, and yes, society demands it. As parents, if we represent the most influential and consistent component in our children's lives, but fail to live up to our responsibility in disciplining our children for their future, we will only gain for ourselves a world that is lawless and out of control. The Bible speaks of such a generation that lived in a time where there was no authority in all of Israel, and the result was "everyone did what was right in his own eyes" (Judges 21:25 ESV). Suffice to say, it wasn't a good moment in Israel's history. And not taking your rightful, authoritative place in your children's lives will not produce a good moment in your own home.

The Power of Common Sense

Like me, you probably find yourself dismayed right now at the display of a serious lack of common sense in almost every facet of our culture. I find myself shocked over and over again almost every single day. I tell myself that I shouldn't be, because having been a pastor for over thirty years, I assumed I had seen everything possible at least once and most things twice.

Look, parenting doesn't take a doctor of education degree, or even an undergraduate study at some university or tech school. A lot of it is pure, old common sense. The "good sense the Lord gave you" as my mother or dad would say. (By the way, I heard my grandparents and great-grandmother utter the exact same phrase. Talk about generational consistency!)

Most of us really do have an adequate storehouse of common sense. It's usually paired with a necessary degree of skepticism and suspicion. That's not a bad thing. As a parent, I can tell you not to be taken in by everything your child says or does. They have an agenda. I had an agenda growing up, and so did you. Now, I was a good child, a primarily compliant child, a responsible first child, and it was generally my mode of operation to obey and not rebel, to tell the truth and not lie, to go above and beyond the call of duty and not be lazy . . . until it served my purposes not to be those things. Then, all bets were off!

When your child comes home, you may ask, "How did your day go?" or "What would the teacher tell me about you if I called her right now and asked her?" This is a moment when your common sense should be on full alert. I did this once with our son Luke.

"How'd your day go, Luke?"

When his response was, "You won't believe it, Dad, but my teacher really likes me!" my commonsense meter redlined.

Something's not right here, I thought. Time to be creative and consistent all at once.

I responded by saying, "Wow, that's great, son, because I've been a bit worried about your grades, but I'm glad she likes you. That should help solidify your grades for sure."

Using consistency in my approach, I did not stop there, but continued. "How do you know she really likes you?"

"Oh," he replied, "she had me move my desk right up next to hers today."

And that's when common sense kicked into full gear!

"Is that right? Right up next to her?"

In my mind I'm thinking, *Yeah right, something isn't right here.* Sure enough, a quick call to the teacher revealed a lot. The teacher explained that Luke is one of the most friendly, like-able, and pleasant students she has. Ten for citizenship! But she went on to explain, "He spends too much of his time talking and making friends and not enough time on his assignments." My commonsense meter paid off. I now knew the answer to the poor grades. I now knew a bit more about his personality and about what areas would need to be reshaped and monitored going forward.

Luke is fantastic with people. Everyone liked him and still does, but he was going to need me and his mother to step in and help him with the discipline of getting his work and assignments accomplished fully and on time. Today, he is a great upcoming leader at a major airline, he consistently gets high ratings and promotions by his superiors, and those under him (when I meet them, as I'm often allowed to do) do nothing but sing his praises as a boss and a leader.

We had a goal in mind for Luke when he was just eight or nine years old in elementary school. We had to creatively discipline and shape him. We couldn't laze out but had to be consistent in our approach with him for as long as he remained in our home. We had to use our common sense at all times, because there was no book available to us to that would even come close to covering every situation and contingency.

Proverbs 3:21–25 says, "Don't lose sight of common sense and discernment. Hang on to them, for they will refresh your soul. They are like jewels on a necklace. They keep you safe on your way, and your feet will not stumble. You can go to bed without fear; you will lie down and sleep soundly." The first time I read that, I couldn't believe how much sense it made in light of what we're seeing all around us these days. It's like common sense has left the building, and we couldn't think our way out of a brown paper sack if our lives depended on it.

Discernment is necessary in parenting. When we were trying to get one past my mother or father, their discernment flag went up, red lights starting flashing, and the storm was about to hit.

Sarah Says

We have had very commonsense solutions placed before us time and time again. One time we had a child who struggled with lying. We had seen it over and over in small things, but we had just discovered this child had lied about cheating on a large portion of their last math book. When we found this out, we had the child repeat the whole grade of math, which was effective in and of itself. However, we soon found another way to drive our point home. Being pastors at our church, I needed to visit a young woman from church who was going to jail to serve time for perjury. What a great time to teach my child a real life lesson! I sat this child down and talked about how this woman had lied and was now going to serve time in jail for a while, in a very general way that was appropriate for the child's age. I was met with very wide eyes. What seemed like an easy way out in the moment could have jail consequences in the future? This lying habit that we had seen several times with this child stopped after this time. I was so grateful for the timing of that situation!

Little did we know as youngsters what was taking place in them. My mother could discern a hidden agenda or a bold-faced lie with the speed of a Formula One racing vehicle. When we were small, she used to attribute it to "a little birdy told me." I used to look for that bird all the time. I had plans to strangle it. Later, as we grew, she brought God into the picture. "God told me" or "God showed me," she would declare. As a teenager, how do you come against an Almighty God who obviously favors your parents over you? I didn't want to end up in hell for all eternity, so I learned pretty early on not to lie. The wise man of Proverbs was right on. Don't lose sight of common sense and discernment. Hang on to them, he states, for they will keep you safe on your way, your feet (that is, parenting) will not stumble, and you can go to bed without fear and be able to lie down and sleep soundly. I don't think my parents lost one night of sleep worrying themselves sick to death over three rambunctious boys. I threatened to run away from home once when I was five. I even did it, with the help of my mother's brother, my uncle. He had more fun toys and things at his house than my parents did. My mother didn't come apart at the seams because I wanted to live with my uncle. She didn't tear up and become an emotional wreck, sobbing uncontrollably into her hanky. She actually helped me in my plans by calling my uncle to come and get me, helping me pack my little suitcase, kissing me good-bye, and walking me out the front door to the corner to await my ride. I think I lasted an entire hour at my uncle's house before I was the one crying that I wanted to go back home where I belonged. I never attempted a run again in my life!

Let me leave with you a true story from history. It seems that at the end of World War II our thirty-third president, Harry S. Truman, was contemplating what punishment to mete out to the Japanese government and its people for the horrible atrocities committed by them during the war. His respected secretary of war, Henry L. Stimson, who would soon be leaving the cabinet and who had urged Truman to show mercy to vanquished Japan, offered his wise counsel. He told Truman, "When you punish your dog, you don't keep souring on him all day after the punishment is over; if you want to keep his affection, punishment takes care of itself."[1] I like that. Punishment takes care of itself. In other words, it needs nothing extra and nothing drawn out. Let it do its job and move forward in the relationship. That advice will work well for you as a parent with your children. Don't be afraid to punish. Just do it, then immediately look for ways to restore the relationship.

A commonsense approach to parenting will save you countless worry lines and wrinkles in your face. Those children you have right now may be getting on your very last nerve. I encourage you to stop, take a deep breath, then approach the problem they're presenting in a creative, consistent, and commonsense fashion. It will always work! You'll find out what my mother knew all along. The Lord God Almighty was always on her side!

Commonsense Applications

- Take an inventory right now and list two or three areas of concern you see in your children that need some immediate discipline and correction. After determining what the areas are, develop some unique, out-of-the-box approaches to bring correction to these areas.

- Discipline is the lifelong training that everyone needs. Are you taking a long-term view to the disciplining of your children? Can you picture them living with the current unchecked or uncorrected behavior when they are in their twenties or thirties? What does that look like?

- Do you find yourself getting tired simply trying to remain consistent? Are you feeling you have to correct every little thing, and it's leaving you exhausted? Try tackling just the main areas of character that you know will produce long-term consequences, such as lying, cheating, stealing, and so on.

If your children don't hate you by the time they're teen-agers, you're doing something wrong.
    —An emotionally intelligent mother or father

CHAPTER FIVE

"Guess Who Wet the Bed?"

The Principle of Healthy Emotional Well-Being
Dealing with Ego, Fears, and Insecurities

Emotional Well-Being

Before you get really upset with me, I don't believe that quote at the top of the page is something to shoot for when raising children. I just tend to think it's a by-product if you're doing things reasonably well. I can't tell you how many times I've heard a very sincere and intelligent mom or dad tell me that their children "are my best friends." You've got to be kidding me. I never thought of my mother or father as my best friend when growing up with my brothers and sister in Detroit. In fact, that's about the last thing I'd call them. Oh, I had friends, to be sure, and during our occasional rumination times we would talk about our parents.

I don't recall ever once the term "friend" being used by any of us kids on the block!

Let me set the record straight right now: you are not raising friends! Maybe, if you do a good job raising them, they will become friends and confidants once they hit their forties or beyond. If you need friends that badly, join a book club. In the meantime, wake up every day reminding yourself that your job is one of parent. Your role is to prepare them for the cruel, hard world of life they will one day possess. With so many societal challenges and such easy access to unhealthy influences, our children must be emotionally fit to navigate the harsh realities and challenges of life. Today, too many are not prepared, and the evidences of that are played out on the news broadcasts every night.

If your child doesn't understand that they will at some point fail, not make the grade, not get the trophy, or not win the competition, then you have failed to prepare them emotionally for life. That reminds me of another emotionally aware saying a mother was heard uttering one day. "Everybody's got to eat a hill of dirt in their life. You might as well get started on yours."

My parents were not aware of the fairly new scientific field referred to as Emotional Intelligence (EQ). It really didn't come into vogue until the mid-1980s. That didn't matter to my folks. They didn't need the training, it just came naturally to them. They knew how to pop the balloon of an overactive ego.

Some of the most memorable times occurred when one of us would occasionally wet the bed. I've heard stories of some parents hanging the wet sheets out the upstairs bedroom window for all to see. My parents never did that, thank God. But typically in the evening around the dinner table, when it was assumed that all the terrible events of the previous night were forgotten and corrected, if our youthful boasting, posturing, and egos had become somewhat inflated during the day, a simple question would be quietly asked by my mother, "Guess who wet the bed last night?" That immediate and sudden ego deflation was so loud, it was like the sound of a mighty rushing wind.

Today, with a culture of perfect air-brushed models alongside increasing legal addictions and the alarming upward trend of suicides, it's imperative that we get this area right. Regardless of whether you manage family stress by tag-teaming as two working parents, by step-parenting, or by shouldering most of the work as a single parent, one thing hasn't changed for decades:

a parent's influence in a child's life is paramount. If you aren't emotionally stable, you won't have the ability to raise emotionally healthy children.

Our Past Influences Our Parenting

There's probably no greater sense of helplessness than when you come to the realization that your deep and committed love for your children will only take you so far. No matter how much you love them, your past hurts, conditionings, and experiences as a child yourself, along with unresolved conflicts and insecurities, will sabotage your best efforts.

There are really only two ways we can move forward. We can deny the impact of our childhood, or we can learn to heal ourselves while supporting our children's growth and enhancing their emotional development. Daniel Siegel, a child psychiatrist and early childhood expert, addresses the effect of our past on our parenting experiences: "Issues that are rooted in our past impact our present reality and directly affect the way we experience and interact with our children even when we're not aware of their origins. To our role of parenting, we bring our own emotional baggage, which can unpredictably interfere in our relationship with our children."[1]

This means actually requiring a breaking of the "power" of our past. Our past is always related to the present, and how the family in which we grew up has a lot to do with how we're put together, how we approach parenting, and how we just live life. There's generally a lot more to us than meets the eye or what people perceive us to be. It's sort of like an iceberg. Deep beneath the surface of our lives are layers of childhood wounds, unconscious motivations and fears, defenses, and memories/experiences we might have even forgotten. Huge chunks of who we are that remain hidden beneath the surface. But they will surface the moment you begin raising children.

Try having eleven children, like my daughter Sarah and her husband, Solo, have. I can tell you, it's fascinating to me how they are all related in so many ways, both physically and emotionally. But if you take the time to talk to and seek to understand each one a little deeper, you will find there is a lot of uniqueness just below the surface. Those attributes expose traits like pride, hurt, anger, amusement, and so forth (the list is never ending), some of which we often can identify as coming from one side of the family or the other.

Do you remember being annoyed or hurt by something that your parent(s) did when you were growing up, and then vowing to yourself, "I will never be like that when I grow up," or "I will never parent like that when I am one day a parent"? Yet, as sure as the sun rises in the east, we find ourselves struggling with the same insecurities, egos, or fears, and the same character defects and unhealthy relational patterns as our parents did. Don't feel bad here. We all have the same problem, and we all have to take the necessary steps to look beneath the surface in our own lives prior to raising our children with the hope they won't have to deal with the same things we do. Now, just a warning: you won't get all the issues resolved. But if you can identify and then address some of the bigger areas and work on those issues, it will help immensely when it comes time to help your children confront them.

These icebergs shape the way we respond, relate, and react to people and situations in our daily living. Working on that particular fear that wants to rise to the surface in your emotions will help you understand how to help your child overcome his or her fears. For example, recognizing that my insecurities at times made me very unsure of my ability to be a lead pastor of a church, caused me for many years to remain in a "behind the scenes" role in leadership. Too often I witnessed the leader taking heat and unjust criticism—I wanted none of it. As I developed the courage to address and confront those insecurities, and to do the real work of inventorying my emotions, I began to mature in that area. I started to realize that my leadership qualities were being reduced or held back by me and, ultimately, I was only thinking about me. I was not thinking of the good of the whole. I found myself finally free to move into a lead role with a confidence that I was able to handle anything from anyone that came my way. That's not arrogance but assurance. Years later, I was able to identify those same insecurities in my children and help them overcome them at a much earlier age than I did. Just remember, God created human beings as complex and intricate creatures. We each have many different aspects to who we are (emotionally, physically, spiritually, and so on), but we also have many different layers. In our everyday decisions, all sorts of motivations, thoughts, and impulses are at work. Some we are conscious of, but others we are not. Our human nature, however, tends to run away from the full truth about ourselves. Don't give into the tendency! It will take courage on your part to confront these undesirable responses in certain situations. It will take courage to ask yourself: "What am I really feeling in this situation? What's really going on here?" This is especially so when you are experiencing a "negative" emotion such as anger, shame, bitterness, jealousy, fear, or depression.

Because none of our childhood experiences was perfect, we all come into adulthood with leftover emotions from those early years. Sometimes this is called "emotional baggage" or "unfinished business." These bags can be heavy and loaded with anger, fear, anxiety, insecurity, resentment, shame, hurt, self-contempt, and so on. My discontentment with my insecurities and refusal to give them room to grow, in the above example, had to be the starting place. It was my unfinished business. I didn't really even realize I was carrying any baggage, and I certainly didn't know what caused it, but dealing with the "unfinished business" when it comes to your own emotional health and maturity will go a long way to help you identify in your children the same issues, and help them walk through them and come out on the other side with a healthy emotional status. This will increase the likelihood of making them successful in their marriage, their studies, their vocation, and yes, the raising of their own children. I firmly believe this helped us three boys immeasurably. My mother did not have an easy childhood in many respects, but she bravely confronted those issues and situations and went on to lead and parent in spite of them.

Now, having looked into ourselves a bit, let's get back to the business of raising our children.

Family Secrets and Commands

Every family has secrets. Yours is not unique in this area. There are a lot of things we know and learn about each other in the home that are never to be shared outside the home. For instance, when one of us boys wet the bed, those sheets were *never* hung out the upstairs window for all the world to see, as was the practice of some. Those episodes were real and could be embarrassing at times, but they were *our* embarrassment and not one single person, family, friend, or enemy outside our home ever knew anything about it. We operated under an unwritten commandment: What happened in the home, stayed in the home.

I don't know about you, but I inwardly cringe whenever I see a parent deliberately embarrass or degrade one of their children in public. First, it lets me know that parent is not emotionally mature themselves, and second, the thought that public shaming or embarrassment will bring about any kind of substantial change is delusional. Lessons are to be learned all through the years your children are in your home. How they are learned is where you come in, but whatever you do, make sure those lessons are learned in a home environment that serves as a secure, safe, and secret workshop where children are planted and grow so they will one day produce a strong new generation of leaders.

Self-Aware Parents

Sarah Says

YouTube is a place where we share aspects of our lives with the world, or whoever cares to watch. We choose to share mostly the highlights of what is happening in our lives out of a deep concern to protect our children and their reputations. Because of this editing, some who watch our videos perceive that we are perfect parents with perfect children. That is just not the case. By the way, that is never the case with anyone. Because there are no perfect people. In fact, I like to say that the longer we parent, the more we realize how imperfect we are—as parents and as people. Children challenge all the things you have not worked on in your life. Things you may not even realize are there. Children are demanding by their very nature. That works on your selfishness day and night. And patience is just a small example.

How do you control your anger? You may think you have it perfectly under control until a child does not sweep the floor after you have asked them to multiple times. Or your teenager walks away from you in a huff and slams the door. Have you experienced something like that? Then you likely know your response is anger. I like to remind myself of the fact that no childhood experience is perfect and everybody has at least a few things they would change about their own experiences. That takes the pressure off! I will make mistakes, and my kids will make their own mistakes as parents and as adults one day. We apologize to our children when we get it wrong, which also demonstrates humility and the willingness to continue to grow. And we believe and hope that they will do the same as the circle of life goes on.

You certainly live in the real world enough to realize that a household with more than one boy in it is going to see conflicts and fights among those boys. That dynamic is just going to increase exponentially depending upon the number of boys that you have. I don't imply that a house full of girls doesn't experience fights—they do. Girls just fight differently than boys. You also will have fighting even if you just have one boy and one girl in the home. I can attest to that in our home with our two children.

In my childhood home, there were three boys. And we fought! Boy, did we ever fight. We would fight silently and secretly. We would fight openly and boisterously. We three boys became extremely good at all forms of fighting and conflict. When I say "fighting," I just don't mean taking a fighter's stance with hands in boxing gloves up in a ring with a buzzer and a referee. First, we never owned a pair of boxing gloves, that I recall, and second, when we fought it was usually immediate and impulsive. There was never any preparation or contemplation of how the fight might go. Emotions of young boys wait for nothing. The only thing the fight did in the immediate is bring to our remembrance all the slights and digs from that particular brother over the last several days, weeks, or months, which in turn justified and propelled us in a greater way to the course of action we were now embarked on.

Such was the home filled with three normal boys. Boys fight. Boys determine their territory, whether that territory is the back seat of your father's sedan or the shared bedroom. Ego, peer pressure, emotional instability, hormones, competitions, jealousy, or any number of things in any given moment or any given combination will potentially produce conflict. That's typical.

What might not be typical is the response of your parents. Our mother was very self-aware. She knew who she was and what role she played. There was no hesitancy or ambiguity found in her. She could respond immediately, decisively, and forcibly when called upon and when the situation warranted it. And it didn't matter what the situation presented or what or who was involved. We always joked that she could control her three boys with just a look. Now that's an art more than a science. If you got "the look" you knew your next few moments of response would determine what your eternity (or at least it could feel like an eternity) would be. If your response wasn't what she was looking for, or worse, if that response yielded even further rebellion on your part, guilt would be declared, sentence would be imposed, and God help you if you debated or repeated the offense.

I don't want to leave you with the impression that every time there was a disagreement or fight, my mother would immediately intervene. The exact opposite is true. I told you she was a very self-aware individual, and I think that helped determine her responses to us boys, as well as keeping her sane. She didn't respond very often to all our bickering, backbiting, and baiting each other. She didn't feel as though she had to intervene in every squabble, snarky remark, or struggle. And unless actual blood-spilling occurred, she avoided interjecting herself in every fight, brawl, and bout. In fact, I remember only one time my parents intervened, when they were convinced my brother Ron and I would probably kill or maim our youngest brother, Mike, if an intervention wasn't initiated. Their solution was to move Mike into his own bedroom for a while and give him a break from the axis of evil represented by our alliance.

Generally, my mother simply kept an eye on things and made sure things didn't get out of hand. Now the brothers are all in our sixties. If asked, we would tell you honestly that, for the most part, she enjoyed—yes, enjoyed!—every interchange.

Instinctively, she knew common relational conflicts built us up as individuals so we began to form and know our own boundaries, as well as learn to respect others' boundaries.

Today, we are peaceable men, and we three are each other's best friends. Being raised by relatively emotionally balanced parents offered us a living example of what we wanted our adult living to look like. As we matured and grew and came into our own, the fighting ceased, but more importantly, the vying and competition came to an end when we were all encouraged and affirmed in our choices (career, marriage, children, and so on) by those same parents. This in turn caused us to experience the same affirmation from each other. We can disagree with each other and still have no problem sitting down together for a meal and laughing our heads off with tales of our childhood antics, or vacationing together with our spouses and having a blast. When I look at the three of us and the few close friends we each have outside the family, the common thread is that those same friends (although rare) have usually been raised the same way—with an ego that's in check, with insecurities that have been battled and fallen, and with a sense of purpose and a strong self-identity that eliminates most fears. Therefore, we easily accept each other's friends into our close circle.

I guess the other guys were raised by the same type of parents we had.

The Five Dynamics of Emotional Intelligence

I just got off the phone with my publisher, complaining about the difficulties I have been having writing this chapter. I have now officially erased more words than I have written. Since I received my doctorate degree in the field of emotional intelligence, I keep getting too technical, which results in getting way out in the weeds.

So, with that bit of self-disclosure, let me offer for you a quick set of crib notes (back in my school, they were called CliffsNotes) outlining what emotional intelligence is all about.

There are five basic components to emotional intelligence: Self-Management, Self-Awareness, Self-Regulation, Self-Motivation, and Empathy. I won't go into each of those five areas in real depth, but each area is important, and more importantly to you the parent, each area must be addressed and developed in your children for their own emotional health and well-being.

Self-Management really isn't anything more than teaching your children how to live in order to be successful in this world, no matter what they eventually choose to do. High school and college will not instill this particular component in your student. If they wait till then, they will have waited too long. This management includes the setting of goals, decision making, planning, and even scheduling. My mother was especially good at this. We were each taught to set goals, then she wouldn't let up until we had completed those goals. The actual goal wasn't important, except that it made us reach and couldn't be too comfortable. When we completed that goal, she helped us analyze and evaluate the way or method we pursued those goals. And God forbid you didn't have any goals, because she would create one, or several, for you!

The way you can help your child master the art of self-management is by teaching them how to do several things early in life. First, teach them **consistency**. That helps them to be stable. The values you hold dear should always be transparent and in place. This lesson will serve them well in their adult years. Always changing your opinion or way of disciplining, on the other hand, not only causes others to question your beliefs but can also cause you to become confused about what you truly believe. Think generationally here. These are how values are passed down from one generation to the next. (For more on values, see chapter 3.)

Second, teach them how to **stick to a plan**. Learning how to complete a given task and making sure it is done in a timely manner helps alleviate your frustrations as a parent when they disregard the plan.

Third, make them **accountable**. There are always going to be times when things don't work out as your children might have planned, but it's important to be able to admit that, then use creativity to get things back on track. My wife is a big proponent of this. She even helped me in this area when we first were married. I hate admitting when I'm wrong, and worse is saying "I'm sorry." Let's say, she cured me of that! The whole idea here is being able to easily self-analyze and then make necessary adjustments and move on. Don't let anything become a defeat that destroys.

Sarah Says

As parents, Solo and I try to consistently teach our kids with the goal in mind of their future self-governance. They need to learn how to make decisions and make mistakes. How to learn and grow with our guidance and then, eventually, on their own. They need to know how to not only seek out counsel and submit themselves to mentorship but also be confident when they know what they need. They need to know how to avoid comparing themselves to others by being confident in who *they* were created to be. We let them make mistakes and navigate relationships while watching and staying involved so that we can coach as need be. One thing I have noticed is that Solo recognizes some of the ego and insecurities in the boys much faster than I do. I may think he is being harsher than necessary on a particular son on a particular day, but in the end, he is usually (always? Ha ha) right about what that boy needs. He sees it more clearly in our sons, and I see it more clearly in our daughters! I have learned to let him carry out what is necessary with the boys. In the end, he has always been right with what he sees, and they respond to his correction much better than I predicted. It is vice versa with the girls.

Recently our oldest son turned eighteen and now has his own phone. He pays the bill and has complete control over what he has on his phone and the time he spends on it. He told me that he has set up parameters for himself, unbeknownst to me. He has timers for how long he can spend on certain apps that are time-wasting temptations. He has multiple screens put in place that protect him from running into pornography. And he has a schedule that he keeps for himself regarding when he will use his phone. I was so proud of him for taking those actions on his own accord. I also recognize these actions come from years of hard conversations and consequences when the cell phone was still a home phone that he had shared access to. In turn, I know that his example with his own phone provides another tool for his younger siblings to learn from.

Fourth—and this is an important point in an ever-changing world—learn how to **educate yourself**. I think my parents did more to help us in this area than they might realize. They didn't let their parental status, age, or level of education keep them from learning. Instead, they embraced change! My mother was an avid reader and unafraid to talk and listen to mentors, peers, young people, and older people. She knew they might know something that could help her along her journey. She taught me to do the same.

A dear, sweet lady in our congregation lived to be 107 years old. She was amazing. Only for about the last six months of her life was she mentally and physically not fully engaged. On the worst snowy Sundays during the Nebraska winters, she would be right on time and right in the front row of the sanctuary. I couldn't even get the twentysomethings to do that. I'm not a medical doctor, but I do think I know what allowed her to live so vibrantly for so long, in spite of a very difficult life. She was flexible and never quit learning. So many people become rigid by their fifties and will not even consider changing or being flexible on issues. (One day I need to write a book about what this woman taught me about life.)

Last—and this is not one of my favorite areas—stay **physically fit**. Many people don't think of staying fit when they talk about self-management, but it is a very important part of being able to practice the four preceding points. A body that is not well rested, nutritionally fed, or physically exercised can lead to emotional and physical illnesses. Take an inventory right now of your children. Are they decomposing in front of the TV or always on the smart phone or computer? Turn off the device and get them outside to play. Are they eating junk food all the time? Consider whether your busy schedule is forcing you to make unhealthy food choices. Try to provide healthy, nutritional meals when possible and leave the junk food at the store.

I learned early on that I was not athletic in any shape or form, and with the encouragement of my parents, I was taught not to compare myself with others, including my two brothers, who played in all sorts of sports. To this day, my brother Mike can do just about anything on a car or home that needs repair, redoing, or renovating. Thank God he now lives close to me as I move into the autumn of my life.

The second big component of emotional intelligence is **Self-Awareness.** My parents helped me discover how to be self-aware, one of the touchstones of emotional intelligence. Being "aware" of one's self is having the ability to accurately perceive one's skills, knowledge, value, and responsibilities. It means learning how to be confident in what you have to offer, whether personally or professionally. Little did I realize how the important lessons in the home and the conversation and debate around the dinner table would prepare me to be emotionally healthy later in my career. I was a church pastor for many, many years, and I can assure you that everyone who is anyone has an opinion on what a pastor "should" do and how he or she should do it. I've never understood why they don't do the same thing with their medical doctor, but who am I to judge? I had to make some hard decisions during those years, and I couldn't make being popular my priority.

Self-awareness is not only important for one's self-esteem but is also the first step to the process of full acceptance or change. Think about it. Without understanding why an individual thinks the way he or she thinks, or acts the way he or she acts, that individual may never fully appreciate himself or see the importance of making changes to improve herself, if necessary. When employed correctly, though, self-awareness gives the individual power and a sense of peace or happiness. This balanced emotional component will carry over into your work life, how you perform your work, and how you interact with others. But when self-awareness is absent, not only will you have doubts about yourself but the people you interact with (or marry, or raise, or lead) and you will begin to question your competence, which ultimately leads to a lack of leadership (read: parental) effectiveness.

Shirley Says

In my experience, I found that often the biggest ego you have to confront is the firstborn's ego. Because they are the oldest, as well as first at experiencing things or given first opportunities, being the firstborn tends to develop a sense of superiority in them. This attitude doesn't start and stop with the oldest but will eventually make its way down through the ranks as long as there is a younger child whom the older child can control. There is a "pecking order" in every family dynamic. The older always assumes they have the authority over the younger.

I used to combat this attitude by deliberately validating the younger one, by making a "big deal" out of the younger child's talent or personal qualities. But don't stop there. Make the older one see the qualities and compliment them too. This practice has a twofold effect. It builds the confidence of the younger and deals with the overaggressive ego of the older. This approach also contributes to making each child more self-aware—the basic building block of emotional health in your children.

Self-Regulation is another term for "self-control," defined as the ability to control one's emotions, desires, and behaviors in order to achieve a positive outcome in all relationships. In this day and age, however, we are so encouraged to "express how we feel" that self-control becomes difficult to practice. There is nothing wrong with expressing how you feel, but there is a delicate emotional balance between expressing one's feelings and avoiding unnecessary tension and conflict. Tension and pressure are by-products of living in a mixed-up world with seven billion other people. Self-regulation is a direct reflection of the type of pressure someone experiences. There are three types of pressure we must teach our children to identify and then control. *Good pressure* is the result of an aggressive yet noncritical and harmless atmosphere, where you can aspire to be like the people you're around. It's motivational, inspiring, and leads to the acquisition of self-regulation. *Bad pressure* happens when the atmosphere is critical and harmful. As a parent, if you are easily triggered in your emotions and you "blow up" with every little slight or hurt, your children will begin to see everything—every decision, every statement, every thought—as directed against them. When that happens, self-regulation is lost. Finally, there is *no pressure*. When an individual is not experiencing any pressure, they tend to act based on emotion, since there is no one to compare themselves to. Have you noticed how many people these days are making life-altering decisions based on emotions? That never turns out well. Emotional decisions made in haste, without deliberation or knowledge, and with the motive of making us feel good in the moment. Feelings come and go and situations can change within minutes, but when you commit your decision to an emotional moment, you run the real risk of living out of control.

Self-Motivation is another component of emotional intelligence. Andrew Carnegie said it best. "People who are unable to motivate themselves must be content with mediocrity, no matter how impressive their other talents are." This component is an essential part of excelling at this thing called life. Teaching your children how to motivate themselves helps them understand they cannot depend on others to do it for them. As a parent, you can help this process, particularly as the children get older. Helping them discover their passions—and how to pursue them and improve at them—is the primary goal here. Teach them how to encourage themselves in a project, for example, and not give up, no matter how bad or difficult the situation is.

Some of the keys to building self-motivation include working toward a cause, avoiding comparing themselves to others, making a conscious effort to persevere, and not living in past failures *or* successes.

Finally, emotional intelligence also conforms our **Empathy**. Empathy is nothing more than sharing in the feelings of others, whether joy or sadness. In order for empathy to work, a child must first be able to recognize, classify, and understand their own feelings. The learned ability to put oneself into the mental shoes of another person and to understand his or her emotions and feelings is almost lost in today's world. In this day of "all about me," empathy is a missing emotion and must be reinstilled in coming generations, or I fear the living unto one's own self will produce the most horrible of earthly conditions.

Shirley Says

I was always looking for ways to encourage my children to get their minds off themselves and onto others. That's a human-nature problem. Thinking of others has the effect of producing a greater level of empathy and fighting that natural tendency toward self-centeredness.

Years ago in Detroit, our three boys had to share a bedroom. This proved to be a benefit.

First, there was never a chance for one child to go off on his own, to his own room, and slam the door and feel sorry for himself. This helped each of them learn how to manage relationships and manage themselves. I figured if they couldn't manage the relationships among themselves, they were certainly going to fail outside the home. This didn't mean that fights didn't break out occasionally between them—there was plenty of that. But eventually they had to stuff down their ego and insistence on having their own way and learn how to go along and get along with others.

What Does Success in This Area Look Like in Real Life?

One of the greatest coaches in basketball history was John Wooden, an English teacher who happened to be the famous coach of the UCLA Bruins basketball team. Long before emotional intelligence was ever developed into a science, he developed his own definition of success that directed him to be a successful leader of future leaders. Those players were his kids, and he helped them to learn more than basketball. Early on, he understood that some parents' measure of success for their children was too often reduced to a performance or a grade. If the student didn't make an A or B, too often parents would make them feel that they, or the teacher, had failed. Coach Wooden understood, however, that the good Lord didn't create all of us equal as far as intelligence (mentally or emotionally) is concerned, any more than we're the same in size or physical appearance.

Coach Wooden taught his students three important principles. First, he taught *never try to be better than someone else.* You have no control over that. Second, *learn from others,* because you can learn something that you didn't know. And the last and most important element is *never cease trying to be the best you can be.* In other words, success is peace of mind attained only through self-satisfaction, knowing you made the effort to do the best of what you're capable.

In explaining his formula for success, Coach Wooden said,

> Don't be thinking about scoring somebody. Let that be a byproduct. This is success: when you have that peace within yourself. If you don't have peace with yourself, you don't have much of anything, and you're the only one that knows that. It's like character and reputation. Your character is what you are—and you're the only one that really knows that. And your reputation is what you're perceived by others, and the two are not always the same.[2]

Coach Wooden described emotional intelligence before the concept became a formal field of study. This is the way to raise healthy emotional and balanced children.

Now, let me not leave you with any false impression. Our mother and father knew very well when we were doing our very best and when we were trying to escape doing the hard work. In other words, if I waltzed in at the end of the school term with a report card filled with Cs and Ds, such low grades weren't going to pass muster in my home. I tried that twice, and it was off to summer school for me in order to retake those particular courses. Inevitably, I would apply myself and pass those courses with a much higher grade. On the other hand, my parents recognized my strengths and weaknesses in these more subjective areas of life. If I brought home a less than good grade in art or shop class, I was given a bit of a pass. They recognized that those skills were pretty much missing in my gift mix. To this day, I can barely draw a stick figure, and I really do hate tools.

Sports was another activity I just didn't enjoy. I participated in track and field and briefly joined the tennis team in high school. Maybe one day I'll share a few stories from those particular endeavors, but I can't right now as I'm still recovering emotionally from the childhood trauma.

Last Word

Remember, as I said from the beginning of this chapter, you do not raise children to have an in-home set of friends. They are your children. You are engaged in molding and shaping them to become mature, balanced, and emotionally stable adults. Your role is to prepare them for the cruel, hard world of life they will one day possess.

As parents, our job ultimately is to raise our children to face an ever-shifting world that is full of conflict, confrontation, emotions, and disappointments. You cannot successfully shelter them from all that and say you prepared them. They won't be ready, they won't be prepared, and the minute—no, the very second—something challenges that sheltered, soft, pablum-filled false reality of life beyond their four walls, you will then suffer the very real truth . . . you didn't prepare them as you should or could.

As we conclude this chapter, let me leave you with a more uplifting little story. There was a famous Jewish rabbi by the name of Zusya. When Rabbi Zusya was an old man, he said, "In the coming world, they will not ask me: 'Why were you not Moses?' They will ask me, 'Why were you not Zusya?'" The true vocation of every human being is, as Søren Kierkegaard said, "the will to be oneself." I take this to mean that maturity in life is when we joyfully live within our God-given limits.

Commonsense Applications

- Think of an iceberg of which we only see 10 percent above the surface of the water. Now take a quick inventory of your own emotional intelligence and ask yourself, what do you normally think of when you consider "going below the tip of the iceberg" in your life?

- It is possible to break free from our past by understanding the families in which we grew up. What areas of your upbringing do you need to break free from?

- How do you deal with the losses in your life?

The single biggest problem in communication is the illu-sion that it has taken place.

—George Bernard Shaw

CHAPTER SIX

"Get the Wax Out of Your Ears!"

The Principle of Good Communication

Can You Hear Me Now?

"Can you hear me now?" was a successful television ad for a large nationwide cell service provider. It could easily have been my parents' byline for most of my childhood and youth, but they instead chose the more direct approach: "Get the wax out of your ears." On occasion, just to mix it up a bit, they would revert to, "Am I not speaking English?" or one of my personal favorites, "Children should be seen and not heard," thereby cutting out communication completely.

Of all the chapters this book contains, this is probably the most difficult one to write, just because it involves a medium—communication—that is totally multifaceted. We communicate, whether we realize it or not, by a multitude of different ways, in the adventure of human interchange. Nothing in our life creates the need for complete, confident, constructed, and critical communication like a home. Trust me on this, without the need to offer up an appendix of firsthand experiences from my years of counseling, pastoring, and yes, parenting.

Almost invariably, any conflicts brought to my office by others with regard to leadership, marital conflicts, or parent-child breakdowns were usually a result of a breakdown of, or a complete absence of, communication. Some people communicated too much, and others—your strong, silent types—couldn't communicate beyond a grunt in front of me when they were the ones asking for the appointment. Those times were always fun!

Shirley Says

Lately, when my husband and I go into a restaurant to eat, we observe there are more and more families who will come in, sit down, order their food and, while they're waiting for it to be brought to the table, sit without even speaking to one another, their eyes locked on their cell phone screens. What's really appalling to us is when, after the food is delivered, they remain not talking but working the phone devices.

I can't understand why families don't feel the need to really get communicating with each other, especially when our culture is as fast-paced as it is, and these moments around the table should be taken advantage of.

How we can spend hours looking and listening to insignificant things, when the most important people in our lives are sitting right across from us, is baffling.

Why not start a new and valuable tradition of eating at least two or three times a week with absolutely no electronics in sight or sound? Then, as a parent, have a list of one or two questions or discussion points that require more than a yes or no response. You will find the experience more rewarding than you could imagine, and you will learn so much more about your children if you will take the time to really listen and offer them the opportunity to talk to you.

You don't need much more than a blank stare and a faraway look to tell you that you're not communicating or connecting. On the other hand, if you think in order to be a good communicator you need to speak with the eloquence of a Winston

Churchill, you are mistaken. As a pastor, most of my job dealt in the art of communication. I had to get really good at it. I took master's-level courses to enhance my vocal communication skills. I feel good that I was a fairly adequate communicator from the pulpit. But communication is not limited to our oratory skill, or lack thereof. We communicate by all sorts of means. Writing, eye-to-eye contact, a touch, a nod, and the list goes on, are all ways to communicate to another human being.

Communicating is one of the most important things we do as a parent. If you have reduced the job of parenting down to barking at your children about what to do and not do, you have probably seriously missed the point of communication. Giving instructions as a parent to your child is not the type of communication I'm referring to. We all do that. For example, "Please get ready for school," or, "You need to watch for cars when you cross the street." If this is all the communication you're doing, eventually this type of communication will only produce a child who will flinch or pull back each time you open your mouth, and who will eventually learn to ignore your orders or pay you only a lip-service obedience.

On the other hand, some parents I've met hugely overcommunicate to their children, as if explaining in great detail their every utterance is endearing them to their children. Nothing could be further from the truth. When you resort to long lectures while engaging with your child, you can almost watch in real time as you lose their attention. In fact, if you practice overexplaining, you may not be aware you are clouding up your communication and making a mountain out of a molehill, as my mother would say. Overcommunication conditions a child to need a full explanation for everything that happens to them in life. Relationship, any relationship, is supported first and foremost by communication. Overcommunication, however, just like undercommunication, can seriously affect relationships.

That won't bode well with your children's future employers, spouse, or other relationships. More seriously, overcommunication feeds natural skepticism, thus eliminating the ability to trust anyone. Unchained skepticism ultimately produces a toxic level of fears and phobias. When communication is a struggle, it can lead to your child checking out emotionally, conflict, and feelings of worthlessness. That's not good preparation for their future.

When you communicate well with your child, however, it leads to a strong relationship, greater cooperation, and feelings of worth.

Closing the Communication Gap

How can parents talk to their children, and in return, encourage their children to become better communicators? How do you get your child to communicate with more than one-word answers? How can you create an atmosphere in the home where they feel free to share thoughts, feelings, and experiences? And more importantly, to share their life with you?

Over the years I have gleaned from the experts—including my mother—some tips I've employed in parenting and pastoring that seem to work pretty well. Let me share them with you as a starting place for you in your parenting role:

Use "Door-Opener" Statements

These statements encourage your child to say more and to share ideas and feelings. They communicate to your child that you are listening and that you are really interested. You show honor anytime you communicate to someone that their ideas are important, and that you accept them and what they are saying. Here's some examples of "door-opener" words or statements:

- "Wow."
- "I see."

- "Oh."
- "How about that!"
- "Really?"
- "Tell me more."
- "That's interesting."

Use More "Dos" Than "Don'ts"

Some children hear a lot of "don'ts." Too often parents know what they *don't* want to happen, so they lead off their communication with a "don't" statement. The downside of that is they fail to promote the positive behavior they're hoping to see. If anything, they reinforce the behavior they don't want to happen. On the other hand, imagine talking to children with a bit more challenge and combine that challenge with an insight into your thinking. You do this naturally with those you consider friends or close acquaintances. So swapping "don'ts" for "dos" might sound something like this.

- "Don't go outside, it's cold" becomes "Stay inside please. It's too cold to play outside today."
- "Don't hit your brother" becomes "Play gently with your brother."
- "Don't color on the carpet" becomes "Please do your coloring on the table."

Now, if they continue to hit their brother after asking them to play gently with them, then I would refer you to chapter 4 on discipline.

Talk with Your Child, Not at Your Child

We all feel rushed in life, and because of that, our default position in communication becomes one of only giving instructions. After all, it takes time to engage in a two-way conversation. Notice I said "conversation," not negotiation or subjugation. Conversation means both talking and listening. This certainly can be challenging when your child has a limited vocabulary or interests, but it's important to practice this fact if you want a healthy relationship now and in the future. Talking *with* your child is a good habit to get into, because when your child is more skilled verbally, they'll *want* to talk with you. When we talk "at" a child, we give the message that their thoughts and feelings are not important or interesting and that the parenting relationship is all about getting the child to do what we want. Besides, if you're a really good questioner *and* a good listener, you'll usually find out more insight on areas of interests in that child or things that need to be addressed concerning that child.

My mother was a master in this skill set. From my earliest days, I can remember standing in front of her as she ironed or prepared dinner. If my answer to her questions "How did school go today?" or "What happened at school today?" was somewhere along the lines of "Oh, nothing really, just a boring day like usual," she wouldn't allow that to stand. "Now, wait," she would implore. "Did you see or talk to anyone on the way?" or "After you got to school, what happened?" or "What did your teacher have to say?" or "After that, what else did she say?"

You get the point. She was relentless, and she didn't just accept my simple answers. She probed and listened and shared her thoughts and ideas. At any given moment in the conversation, she affirmed, corrected, encouraged, role-played, diagnosed, strategized, and game-planned us. She did this faithfully with all three of us boys. Thinking back on it, one of the tougher challenges each of us had with our wives was that we wanted to tell our mother everything from our day, but often didn't say much about anything to our wives. After all, our wives just didn't know how to ask the right questions Mother did!

Sarah Says

Growing up, my parents were wonderful at pulling information out of me. I would come home from school and get all the questions. They knew about my friends, teachers, classrooms, and extracurricular activities. They asked a lot of questions, took interest, and followed up on things they had asked previously. I know they got their skills from my grandparents. Most of my childhood, we did not live in the same city as my grandparents, but they still knew our lives well. They would call us and ask a lot of the same questions! Our grandparents living half-way across the United States knew the names and personalities of our friends and even *their* crushes! They took genuine interest in our lives. They asked questions, remembered the answers, and came back later to inquire on how things had turned out. I love that I had such great examples in both my parents and grandparents. It makes dinner table discussion times fun and interesting every day. Well, some days the young ones are loud and it is hard to get words in, but most days we have a great conversation that is much more memorable than the food we ate. Our kids know we are interested in their thoughts on current events, their friends and current plans, and their ideas about their futures. We want to hear it all! And as they have become teenagers, we have learned that those one-on-one conversations usually happen at night. When they happen, we have to be attentive. Electronics get turned off when they are ready to talk. They have our full attention.

This week, I spent time with my grandma while working on this book together. When we sat down for a lunch break, she immediately began asking about my children. She knows them and their personalities, and she had questions. She is genuinely interested even though she has many great-grandchildren to keep up with! She loves to hear about their strengths and weaknesses and dream with me about what they will be when they grow up. The parenting never ends!

Make Requests Important

Asking if a child would like to do something but being vague in your request is a recipe for causing your child to ignore you. In order to make sure your requests are heeded, you must first ensure you have your child's attention. Then speak with firmness and directness to show that you mean what you say, then give the child (when appropriate) a reason why they must do this thing at this particular time.

For example, if your child is engaged in play, it can be hard for them to shift attention to you, so you might have to work a bit to engage your child's attention first in order for your request to be successful. A successful request would look something like this: "Son, I need you to pack away your toys that are on the table now, please, because we're getting ready to eat and we need space to eat on the table." That's much better than, "Can you pack away your toys? I've already asked you twice."

Use No Unkind Words or Labels

When I'm out and hear a parent berate or label a child, it's like someone has dragged their fingernails across a blackboard in front of me. I'm a pretty outspoken guy and it usually takes everything in my power, including but not limited to biting my tongue and drawing blood, to keep my mouth shut and my opinions to myself. If you want to practice a very *unhealthy* way of communicating to your children, try using ridicule, shaming, or name-calling as a form of communication. I call this kind of communication child abuse.

Statements like, "You're acting like a two-year-old" or "You're embarrassing me" can produce exactly the opposite results you are looking for in a good parent-child relationship.

Using those types of phrases as a means of controlling behavior makes you ineffective and, worse, you lower yourself to that two-year-old level. Remember, parenting is a mind game. You're smarter than they are, and you're smarter than you think.

First, remember that behavior modification begins at home. So do your primary work there. If you do, you won't have nearly so many problems in public which could prove embarrassing to you. Also, use peer pressure in a good way. Don't make a statement like "You should act more like your brother. He's good!" Better to say, "I know you and you have more than this to offer" or "I know you, and you can be better than this." We only had two children, and pitting one against the other would have been an easy response to fall into but would have produced a great deal of harm. An example of using peer pressure in a right way is setting a goal of being better or a leader among friends generally. In other words you're wanting to bring the best out of them and see themselves as capable of changing. That's true behavior modification.

Let me relate to you an episode that happened just a few months ago. We had both our children and their children with us over the holidays for the first time in forever. One morning, we all decided to go out to a restaurant for breakfast. For our family, that means six adults and twelve (at the time) grandchildren ages one through sixteen. As the patriarch of this crazy mob, I knew a restaurant represented a bit of a challenge to our ability to corral behaviors, noise, and confusion. Just getting out of the car in the parking lot showed me that this could quickly deteriorate into a three-ring circus, with me looking like a clown.

Here's what I did to head everything off at the pass. I had all the kids line up in a row from tallest to shortest (except the baby of course) and follow the leader—me—into the restaurant. The children were told to stay in perfect line and to not say anything because we're getting ready to march in as a family. I always like to live by example—call it first-child syndrome. I knew people already in the restaurant, seeing this many children entering the place where they were enjoying a pleasant meal, might feel their peace was about to be threatened, or at least disturbed. Well, the older ones caught on right away, and the younger ones, because of peer pressure, fell right in line. Once a table for eighteen people had been set up, off we marched. No one said a word. Everyone stayed in line, and we blew the staff and clientele right out of the water! The kids loved this act of family unity because they were taking pride in being a part of a bigger deal than just themselves. Additionally, I scattered the little ones among the older ones at the table, and the little ones were so happy to be on the receiving end of the big ones' attention that they obeyed and behaved splendidly. Success!

I even had them pick up after the meal around their chairs. They also helped the wait staff clear the table, then we lined up and marched out the same way we came in. Nobody was embarrassed by someone else's behavior, no one had any meltdowns, and there was no confusion, no mess, and not too much fuss. Best of all, six adults sitting at one end of the table got to eat a wonderful meal in peace.

This feat wouldn't have been possible unless behavioral patterns had already been set at home. The children knew how to respond correctly to an adult—me—without questioning or rebelling. The challenge of the entire family eating out brought out the best in everyone, and we didn't leave the place in shambles or anger the management. I clearly communicated to those twelve children what I expected them to do. I presented a challenge they could all latch on to. I enlisted the older ones to help us make a splash and a positive impression. I summoned the younger ones to a new level of thinking and response that didn't make everything about them. And I did it all without raising my voice or threatening them within an inch of their lives.

Now, I can almost hear your thoughts reading that little story. "What if they had carried on poorly?" or "What if they hadn't listened?" or "What if the restaurant was left in shambles? What would you have done?" Simple. I would have turned to the parents and said, "What kind of behavior are you teaching my grandchildren at home? Do I need to come and live with you for a while, and remind you how you were raised?" (I would threaten that last, but never do it. They're on their own with that hot mess.)

Use Kind Words

Kind words create a good relationship and better communication with your child. Children who are spoken to with appreciation and respect also have better self-worth, which allows them to thrive. Instead of, "You idiot, I told you that would break if you played with it outside," it is better said, "I'm sorry that your toy broke. That probably happened from taking it outside. Let's get the dustpan and clean it up together." Trust me, after a couple of times of doubting you and then living through the consequences they will have learned a great lesson, and you didn't even have to yell or put them down in order to teach it. I'll bet the next time they hear you say, "Play with that inside and not out," they will do so.

A few other examples of kind words:

- "Thank you for helping me with the dishes."
- "You did a good job getting your room cleaned."
- "That really makes me feel good."

- "I like seeing you play nicely with your sister."
- "I love you."

All of these, except the last, might point to things you asked them to do or expected them to do. It's still important that they hear from you a kind word of affirmation. Generally speaking, they really want to please you, but they need to hear communication from you that they are on the right track. Yes, even that daughter in junior high with a chip on her shoulder and an attitude that seems to say to you, "I despise the very ground you walk on."

King Solomon, who happened to be the wisest man to walk the earth, said it like this: "A gentle answer deflects anger, but harsh words make tempers flare" (Proverbs 15:1). And then, because he couldn't leave things alone, he went on to write, "The tongue of the wise makes knowledge appealing, but the mouth of a fool belches out foolishness" (v. 2). I try to be wise, particularly the older I get.

Sarah Says

Solo and I make a point to encourage and affirm our kids more than we correct them. That sounds easy at first, but practically speaking, when you are moving through a day trying to get things done and make things happen, directing and correcting can come a lot easier than praise. But when we look intentionally for ways to compliment and praise the things that child is doing well, it goes so much farther. Yes, children need correction, but they actually take that correction better when they know you are on their side. You believe in them. You *like* them! Not in the "I know you can do better" type of sentence, but in the "You are doing this thing so well!" type of way.

I love to joke with and tease my kids, and they know my personality and temperament well. I will often see something they are doing and tell my child that they are my favorite one that day. Keep in mind I have eleven children, so being the favorite out of eleven is a big deal! They know I don't really have favorites, and I make sure to dish out that title to everyone as often as possible. But when I say it, I really mean it! And it is a fun way to recognize them for the ways they have gone above and beyond. I understand not everyone would be comfortable with such words, but it works in our house because my children know I don't really have a favorite child over-all. A few times I have let that statement, "Wow, Noelle, you are my favorite child today!" stay in a YouTube video we make. Each time I notice several comments of people who wished they could have heard that just once from their parents in their own large family growing up. Children need to feel seen, valued, and appreciated. It is worth finding every creative way to do that!

Other Forms of Communication

When it comes to the issue of communication, there has to be an understanding of why it's important. Communication is used to relay values or knowledge or endearments or any number of things. However, one of the most important ways it's used in the parenting paradigm is the training that tells the child for every action there is a consequence. Rules without relationship leads always to rebellion. So, if you are only always communicating rules (which are important, to be sure) but not taking time to build relationship through communication, eventually that child (or person, or voter, or congregant, and so on) is going to rebel. The area of communication we continue to ignore is the "listening" component. Personally, if I feel someone is listening to me, then I feel respected. This desire for respect is not mitigated just because you're dealing with a child. My ability to listen closely to my child on a consistent basis provides a wholeness in our relationship which, in turn, allows that child to feel free to bring me their "problem." Granted, their "problem" may feel almost insignificant when measured against the problems you are dealing with in any given moment. But parents typically tend to treat their children's problems too lightly. Although their problems don't seem as deep as yours, remember, they don't have the experience you do. So naturally their problems seem deep to them, and thus worthy of your undivided attention.

As you work to improve communication skills in yourself and in your child, may I suggest you keep in mind the following rules of the road. First, hear the child out. All the way. Let them express totally what they are trying to say to you. Which leads to the number two rule: don't interrupt. Wait for the whole story. Our impatience, lack of time, or lack of enthusiasm make us want to cut their story short or fill in the pauses with our own take on the issue being presented. Remember, please, it's not your story! It's theirs! Let them own it. And lastly, could I, in all kindness, speak to some of you wonderful Christian parents a little word to the wise? Whatever you do, don't start quoting Bible verses back at them. It's not that what they are facing doesn't have a wonderful answer found in Scripture, but the regurgitating of some scripture verse to address their important issue shows a total lack of empathy and even tends to make you appear to be a Pharisee. (Really. Look it up.) There will be time later for a great Bible study.

I recognized there were times in my schedule when a child needed to talk, yet my day's calendar was already full. As often as possible, I would delay the next meeting or call I was expected to accomplish and shove those responsibilities aside to give at least a few moments of time to my child. They knew to interrupt me if it was important, and my staff knew to allow them to interrupt. On rare occasions, because of an impossible moment I was having, I would respond, "I want to discuss this with you, but I can't right now. Can you come back or call back in forty-five minutes? Then I'll be able to give you my full attention." I never just said, "We'll talk about this later." I knew I'd be lying, because "later" would have its own demands. If I left it till later, I might forget.

When it comes to other forms of communication, let me remind you to listen with your eyes as well as your ears. My mother excelled in this. She could get a take on our day at school simply by looking at our body language. If my shoulders were a bit slumped, or if I was dragging my feet and moving slow, I could usually expect an "Okay, what happened in school today?" On the other hand, if I wouldn't look her in the eye when she was talking to me or asking a question, I could usually count on an "Okay, young man, you're not giving me the whole story. I want the whole story right now, so start over at the beginning and don't leave any details out."

Sarah Says

My parents took great interest in what I took interest in as a teenager. In my case and my brother's, it was my dad who really dug into our interests and got involved. Up until our teen years, our mother had been naturally involved in a lot more of the day-to-day parenting, but the teen years gave our dad a chance to become more involved. I was very interested in overseas missions, and my dad took me on several trips to different parts of the world. He would sit and talk and dream so much with me about missions!

Although Mom can fill in this role in the teen years, if Dad is around, I believe that his influence and involvement in the teen years can make a huge difference in a young person's life. Solo and I have been finding such fun ways to connect with our kids as they are in those teenage years. Sometimes we already share common interests with our teens. In other instances, we are stretching ourselves to learn, read, and get involved in new things for us. But it is a fabulous way to connect with teenagers and makes for some of the best chances for great communication.

The way a child uses their eyes and gestures is a huge communication tool. If you don't watch and pay close attention, you will miss some of the most important parts of communication. Additionally, I've always found that communication is made so much easier if you are involved together in something you enjoy. I am a private pilot and, early in his teens, I got my son involved in going up with me in a plane. Sitting in that right-hand seat next to me with his earphones on was a thrill not only for him but for me as well. I found out he loved it. So much, in fact, that he went on to take lessons and achieved his private pilot's license at just sixteen years old, the very youngest you can get your license. He's actually a better pilot than I and nothing could make me prouder. That flying time also gave us a wonderful chance to communicate about all sorts of different things and, most importantly, gave me a chance to see and listen to what made him "tick." I didn't have to throw darts of communication up on a board, so to speak, and hope some of them found their mark. I was involved in something he enjoyed, and it opened all sorts of doors relationally between us. To this day, we can still get on the phone with each other and pick up a great conversation just where we left off. Now, he's doing the same thing with his son. That's cool!

Unifying Your Family

Unifying your family and its values is really the ultimate goal of communication. I am not just getting a child ready for that big, bad, and crazy world out there, but I am seeking to develop lasting relationships with some of the most important people on the face of the earth to me—my family. Dogs and other pets will come and go, and so will certain relationships at work or play. However, the relationships I've been given by God within the framework of my immediate family are what I want to work for and must work for during my lifetime. I can't make a member of that immediate family choose to remain in a lasting relationship with me. They have a free will, and I can't interfere or change that. However, as a father and parent, I can employ some basic foundational concepts that will lay a necessary foundation for the potential of such relationships.

My goal is to see my children grow and achieve greater things than I have done. I want to see them succeed in worship, work, marriage, and children. I am their first mentor in accomplishing that. So let me quickly list the areas and corresponding actions I need to take to ensure that these relationships have a fighting chance of lasting throughout my lifetime and the lifetime of subsequent generations.

They first have to know and understand what unconditional love is. It's the basic foundation for a solid relationship. Unconditional love is the same foundation God uses in dealing with you and me. His love toward us is unconditional. Let me unpack that for you.

Unconditional love means to love someone no matter what they look like, no matter the assets or liabilities they bring to the table, and no matter how they act. I am not too old to remember how I acted toward my parents on (brief) occasion. (But I'm way too embarrassed here to confess any of that.)

I know I have to love my children even when I detest their behavior. Now, depending on the situation, this emotion can be very hard to feel and certainly to show, but the closer you can come to this 100 percent of the time, the more confident you will feel. This requires some very good transparent and honest communication. You address the problem, you listen to their response, you reflect on what they've said—excuses and all—and then you determine an intentional course of action. That's part of parenting. I get that. But you still let them know through word and deed that you love them. Children who are loved unconditionally feel good about themselves, and, this may surprise you, but they generally learn quicker from their mistakes in that atmosphere.

Come on, admit it. I'll bet you're exactly like me. At a certain point in your teenage years when serious emotional and physical development was overtaking you, you thought to yourself, "I surely am adopted! I don't belong here. I don't know who these people are, and I'm sure they don't know who I am." The most important question in a teenager's mind is "Do you love me?" They don't realize that, but they ask this primarily through behavior rather than words. They have emotional tanks—needs that need to be met through love, understanding, discipline, and so on. The level of that "tank" determines how they feel and act and what they say. They desperately need full tanks to feel the security and self-confidence they must have to cope with peer pressure and other demands of adolescent society.

There isn't a child in the whole, wide universe who doesn't strive for independence. They do things by themselves, go places without family, and test every rule. But they will eventually run out of emotional "fuel" and come back to parents for maintenance and a "refill." So don't worry if they aren't communicating with you like you'd expect them to or are ignoring your attempts to reach out. It's okay. That short season won't last, because you've built a different foundation that doesn't push away or ignore. If you overreact every time something goes wrong, it will eventually cause you more problems than the original problem. It will then be extremely difficult, or sometimes even impossible, for the child to return to the parents for that emotional "refill," and they will go to peers or others instead.

Secondly, your children have to hear you say, "You are important to me." Not just that simple statement, but variations on that statement, and all the time. "I love you. I care for you. I want you to become God's maximum young man or woman. I am committed to help you be the best that God wants you to be. I will be praying for you. I am here if you ever need a listening ear. I am prepared to make certain sacrifices if it is necessary to help you." Those and other statements go a long way in establishing the worth of that child. They need to know you support them even if they've lost at something. We all like winners, but it's in the low times we find out how much we are really loved. Our suggestion here (and yes, this is from all three of us) is to make it a point to give each family member your undivided attention at least once a day!

The third foundation in building a unified home is humor. I love this one. I love a great laugh, and I love being in a home or around people and families who love to laugh. Sometimes I find parents take themselves too seriously. Every situation becomes a matter of life and death. Stop that! We have too much of the world trying to put that on us and our lives. We shouldn't be self-inflicting here when it's just not necessary. Home should be a fun place. Think about communicating in a different way to achieve this. Tell a story or ten from your childhood—not to just teach a lesson, but to let your children see the real you and get a good laugh. Go through old scrapbooks, photo albums, and so on. Take crazy family pictures.

This may be hard for some of you, but be vulnerable and talk about the silly things you did.

Recently, all our children and grandchildren were together. Years ago, my brother and I had put together a DVD of old 8mm movies from the 1940s through 1960s of my grandparents and their families, my parents and their children, and cousins by the dozen. I got that DVD out and played it. My grandchildren were enthralled and captivated. You could have heard a pin drop in the room. Plus, the videos provided the best couple of nights we've ever had of telling stories and reminiscing about our heritage. All of a sudden, those grandchildren found out they were part of something much larger than they had even realized.

Learn to enjoy your children and grandchildren.

When you think about home, it should be fun. Home ought to be a place where you want to spend time. Being at home with your family ought to be a blast!

Here's another communication mantra that unifies the home: Honesty is the Only Policy. It's not the *best* policy; it is the *only* policy you should have. Letting your children know you are hurt sometimes gives them the needed support when they experience failure or setbacks. Seeing your vulnerabilities shows them you are human, and you have a great beginning point for the honesty-only policy. Now, I don't think you have to gush out every little time you mess up as a parent. But when you are honest about fears and uncertainties, when your kids witness you showing grace under pressure, and when they hear your willingness to communicate about those times, they won't be so shocked when they step into adult life. They will be much better able to deal with conflicts.

There's another area that is often overlooked: family respect. This starts with good communication. Now bear with me for just a moment while I slip into my clerical robes. Our relationship with the Lord Himself is not based primarily on His authority as God, but rather on His love for us. The exact same is true with our children. Know who is boss (you are, as the parent, if you're wondering), but also know that love is the primary building block in your home. A loving relationship is the oil that makes authority tolerable.

Parents need to respect their children (especially teens). It's easy as a parent to set *our* ambitions too high, then find ourselves disappointed with *their* choices. Allow them to be unique individuals as God made them to be. This means communicating your affirmation to them, about them. On the other hand, this doesn't reduce your authority whatsoever in their lives. The most difficult tension you can experience in respecting teens comes when you know that what they are doing will lead to trouble. When you've issued a warning and it proves ineffective, then the most effective thing you can do is communicate the history and the experience you know to be true.

How does that look? Let me give you an example. Say your seventeen-year-old has collected for himself four vehicular tickets, has been in three minor accidents, and doesn't seem to think it should make a difference to you when he comes and asks to borrow the car again. Here's how this usually plays out: You say no. He says, with a sad or mad face, "You don't trust me." Which means, in other words, "You don't respect my request as you should." Your response? "True, son, for the time being you can't be trusted with the car. However, I still trust you in other areas. Continue to grow in those areas and we will revisit the car thing."

Communicating your message in some form shows both your authority—you know what's best at the present time—but also does not minimize or dilute your respect for that teenager.

Last, remember why communication is such an important foundation in unifying your family. It develops family loyalty. Whether you believe it or not, just because a child carries your last name or sits around you dinner table, you still aren't guaranteed to see the development of family loyalty. It takes a certain amount of "quantity" time in order to produce "quality" time. In a totally unpredictable fashion, every once in a while the beautiful moment occurs in the family life. Memories like this produce the glue that binds us together as a family. Family loyalty is the natural outgrowth of a family that practices good communication. Test this yourself. Ask your child or teenager about their most vivid memory. Most likely something you did with them will be recounted. It may have seemed like a little thing to you, but that memory—be it a birthday, holiday, special event, or even something just from everyday living—will build a loyalty to family you will be thankful for in the days and years to come.

Let me leave you with an example I know about, but didn't happen in my family. The story goes that one son of a certain family was away at college but not living a very exemplary life. In fact, by all appearances, it seemed he had thrown out every value he had ever learned in the home and was about to throw out his very integrity and character. One of his brothers—same family, same values, same loyalty—showed up at the college and confronted his older brother and told him, "You are not acting like my brother." That older son started to weep on hearing that concern from his younger brother. He decided, on the spot, to change, but not because of knowing that what he was doing was hurting himself. In fact, he was weeping because he had a strong desire not to do anything to hurt the family. That is representative of the unity God wants for your family (yes, the clerical robe is still on). God can increase your communication skills so you can achieve just that. Just ask Him.

Commonsense Applications

- Think about how you can be more intentional with your communication. Do a self-inventory and see if you're making more statements than asking questions.

- Commit to finding the time each week (calendar it for yourself, if needed, then protect that time) to engage each child in some meaningful communication. Ask a couple of probing questions, then find ways to talk, encourage, and envision your child based on the answers you've been given.

- If you have a quiet or more introverted child, look for ways to spend some extra alone time with him or her and don't let them get away with a shrug or a simple yes or no answer to your questions. It might take a little effort and a lot of consistent meetings before they really begin to open up, but this consistency will prove beneficial to your relationship in the long run. Remember, it's not a sprint but a marathon race you're in.

Nobody ever drowned in his own sweat.

—Ann Landers

CHAPTER SEVEN

"Work Hard, Play Hard"

The Principle of a Strong Work Ethic

The Mantra

"Work hard, play hard." That was my father's favorite thing to say. It was his mantra. Looking at several different definitions of this word, I can paraphrase and offer that "mantra" is a word, formula, or phrase that is repeated over and over again, *often as a truism.*

Well, to my dad, that statement was a truism. I'm sure he learned his strong work ethic from his father, uncles, and grandparents, but he was bound and determined to pass it on to his sons.

My dad only attended one year of college, then joined the army and served most of his time there as a military police officer. During that time, he and my mother married and were stationed in Germany following World War II. Upon their return home and his leaving the army, my father was hired by the Detroit Police Department as an officer, and he worked in that position for thirteen years. I am the oldest (conceived during that time in Germany) and still have such fond memories of Dad getting dressed in his uniform and heading off to work. Every once in a while, he and his partner would drive by the house in their squad car to check in at home or something, and we children, along with the neighbor kids, would get a huge thrill when they turned on the lights and sirens. In our little neighborhood, three other fathers were also cops, so it was a rather tight-knit community.

It was during these years of his employment as an officer that his meager salary just wasn't cutting it for a growing family in Detroit. I suppose my mother could have generated some extra household money if she had gone to work, but back then, working mothers were highly unusual, as typically the mother and wife stayed home and took care of the home and the children. So my father's solution was to find a second job. He began working for a company that produced and sold "baby pictures." (They probably did photos of whole families, but that's how we boys referred to the job.) Dad worked eight hours a day, five days a week, as a police officer, then usually another six to eight hours a day selling those baby pictures. Makes for a long day and a crazy schedule, particularly when you consider that his shift work as an officer would float every three months. In other words, for three months he'd work days, then for three months, afternoons, followed by three months on the midnight shift.

Here's my point. My dad was a hard worker (still is, actually) and he knew how to adequately provide for his family. He understood the task and responsibility handed to him as the head of his home and primary income-producer. He didn't resent this position or the responsibility it incurred, nor did I ever once hear him complain or grouse about how tired or exhausted he was, and he surely must have had those times or even hated aspects of his job. I never remember hearing him complain about his work or the bosses, none of that. I think he took great pride in his work and the responsibilities that were given to him. During this time period, he served as the general contractor on a new house he and my mom built for our family, and he also served in various capacities in his church, got together frequently with his extended family members, and always had time for his wife and children. After thirteen years on the police force, he finally left and changed to a whole different career—insurance sales. He found out through those years of selling baby pictures that he was a natural-born salesperson, and he really enjoyed it. He can sell anything, even to this day.

My brothers and I have all concluded that not one of us ever felt we were lacking or had gotten the short end of the stick when it came to his involvement with us. We still went on vacations together. We still went with him up to a cabin in the north woods of Michigan where we boys hung out, ran around the woods naked like a bunch of lunatics, and learned how to shoot guns and hunt for little animals. We still felt he gave each of us the time and energy necessary to have a huge impact on developing our character and values so that we would carry on the same legacy to our own families one day.

Now, I already mentioned that his mantra was "work hard, play hard." Before my development and in my early teens, my mantra was found more in the book of Psalms and Proverbs of the Bible. My favorite scripture as a young teenage boy was the familiar Twenty-third Psalm: "The LORD is my shepherd. . . . He makes me lie down in green pastures. He leads me by still waters." And when reinforcement was necessary—and it's always important to pull out Scripture in a Christian home—I would turn to Proverbs 6:10 (NIV): "A little sleep, a little slumber, a little folding of the hands to rest." The wonderful words and phrases, *lie down in green pastures* or *a little sleep or little slumber* spoke to me so powerfully. The problem with that is, my dad looked up that passage one day and read the next verse (v. 11) which says clearly, "And poverty will come upon you like a robber and want like an armed man." Soon after that, I quit using the Bible for getting out of work and just went ahead and got to work.

My dad worked hard, and he played hard. He showed us how to enjoy life with both work and play. He exhibited for us a work ethic that said, "You don't quit till the job is done, and you do that job to your best ability." You still can't learn work from just watching other people work, however. You've got to eventually motivate yourself and get out there and learn the discipline and reward of hard work. Lessons of life in this area have to be learned. Let me give an example for you how this happened in my life.

The Detroit Shopping News

When I was growing up, there was a paper that was delivered twice a week to every home in Detroit. At around age fourteen, I took on a job as a paperboy for this newspaper. Up to that point, I had already been given plenty of chores and responsibilities at home to prepare me for work. Lawn mowing, weed pulling, car washing, gardening, sweeping out the garage, picking up the dog poop, cleaning the unfinished basement, and more were all jobs that were given to me at one point or another. Most of them I hated, to be honest, so when the opportunity to do something else, something where I could actually earn some real money, came along in the form of a paper route, I took it.

The company would deliver about two hundred papers to the house in a bundle on Monday night and Thursday night. It was my responsibility to fold those papers tightly so I could carry them in my delivery bag and toss them onto porches. The work was tedious as well as dirty. Do you know how black your hands can get from the ink when folding two hundred-plus papers?

The day after folding was delivery day. To deliver newspapers to two hundred homes is quite an undertaking, representing a number of neighborhood blocks to walk. I had to walk because each house had to receive a paper, and my bags were so full and big, there was no way to fit them on a bike along with myself. So I would walk up one side of the block and down the other, tossing the papers onto the porches. Lots of walking, lots of papers, lots of weight on my shoulders. This job took about two to three hours, on average.

All was going pretty well, however, because I had started the route in the springtime. Winter was a different story. I don't know if you've ever lived through a Detroit winter, but they can be harsh and cruel. It was while delivering papers during one of these hard winter days that I made two rather significant decisions. One was to somehow live out my days in Florida, if I ever got the chance. I'm doing so now. The other was to devise a way to make it "look" like I had delivered the papers without having to walk nearly that far or long.

See, the company had supervisors who would come along and check on you every once in a while to see how you were doing. Well, since I considered myself something of a fourteen-year-old genius, I figured the best way to accomplish my goal of reducing the walk through the snow and ice and still make sure the supervisor would find papers delivered when she checked was to route my travels so I only delivered the papers to the homes at the end of each block on both sides, and just skip all the middle homes in the block! After I got done doing the end homes, I would walk over to a nearby grocery store and drop the remaining papers in their garbage bin. Genius, right?

Well, after about three or four cycles of this, homeowners began to complain to the company they weren't getting their biweekly *Shopping News*. Their complaints brought out the supervisor, who only needed to do a little investigating work to find out my system. She even found the dumped newspapers at the grocery store trash bin. Looking back on it, I realize now I wasn't the only one who had ever tried this. This lady had probably experienced this same playbook with others. So she dug them out of the bin and brought them to my house. Caught!

Well, you can imagine the trouble I got in for this "genius scheme." I was found out, which was humiliating enough, but I had really disappointed my father too—a feeling I didn't enjoy. His response was to make me apologize to the supervisor and beg to keep my job. He also required me to take those papers and go to each home that had been missed. Where possible, I had to personally hand the homeowner their paper, apologize for being late, and say, "It won't happen again, I promise."

Thankfully, that was the last lesson on having a good work ethic that I ever needed in my life. I learned a hard lesson with that little episode. I had agreed to the job no matter the weather conditions, I had agreed to be paid for a certain work performance, and I had agreed to be responsible and trustworthy. I had failed at all three things. I was really upset with myself for a number of days. Not that I had gotten caught, but that I had let so many people down, especially my dad and family.

It's Not All About Money

I do recall finding the ability to make more money appealing with the paperboy job. Up to that point I had been collecting an allowance from my parents for completing chores and assignments around the house. Now, with a paper route, the chance to make big dollars (everything being relative) appealed to my avarice. In retrospect, I don't think I came up with my scheme to *not* deliver papers for the purposes of making money without working for it. In my case, it was more a matter of not enjoying the work.

Over the years, in order to provide for myself or my family, I have had to do some jobs that I simply didn't like or enjoy. They weren't going to become a career choice by any stretch. On the flip side of that coin, however, I have learned I am a much happier human being when I'm working at something I really enjoy or that brings me a great sense of satisfaction and fulfillment. On rare occasions I have even found jobs that were so enjoyable and fulfilling, I almost felt like I was cheating the person paying me. Little did they know I would have worked for free (well, almost) just to be doing what I found myself doing in those seasons in my life.

Sarah Says

I grew up serving others. We served at church. We cleaned buildings and took people meals and had company over and over and over again. We played our violin and cello in nursing homes and retirement centers and at funerals more often than I can count! Service as a family was a huge part of our lives when we were kids, and it has been important to both Solo and me that we also find many ways to serve others together. We have so much fun playing together, whether that is on a vacation, traveling the world together, or just an evening in front of a movie that we remember from our childhood and want to introduce our kids to. But we also really enjoying serving people! Our older children are so happy to volunteer for service opportunities through the church. They will sign up to work in an area on Sunday mornings and will be the first to help a young family move or drive an older person to an appointment when needed. But we also actively find ways to serve people as a family because working together is a great bonding opportunity for us, as well. It also gives us a chance to see up close and personal how our kids work and how they work with other people. We value working together so much that this past year we took some extra time to devote each week just to look for opportunities to serve others as a family. Sometimes it is hard to figure out what we could do next, and sometimes it has required some creativity, but it has been a fun experiment that has hopefully blessed some other people along the way.

Although this chapter isn't about personal finances, economics, or stewardship, I should mention that learning about the value of money, its importance, its power, as well as its place and priority in our life should be something we teach our children. Experiences, the purchase of things we want, savings, and long-term investments, all should have the principle of "work hard, play hard" connected to them. Think about it. If we give our children everything they want, immediately when they want it, thinking we're in a position to not let them experience any lack, we will actually spoil their ability to process the fundamentals of hard work, delayed gratification, and the gift of receiving the rewards from a job well done.

Having the income from that first job allowed me to experience the sheer joy of saving for, then buying, my first indulgence—a transistor radio. Most kids today wouldn't even know what I am talking about, but to have the ability to plug in my little earphone into my brand-new, portable, full-band-plus-short-wave, turn-wheel-dial, with-collapsible-antenna-for-better-reception GE transistor radio with carrying case, and listen to a Detroit Tigers ballgame, or my favorite radio stations, anytime day or night (even when I was lying in bed, supposedly sleeping) represented total freedom for me at fifteen. What made the radio even more enjoyable was that I had saved for and purchased it myself, having done the necessary planning and research on just the right model and size. Not only did I take pride in my earning ability, I also learned that when I purchased something with my hard-earned money, I kept much better care of that thing, so that it would last a long time.

To this day when I purchase an automobile, I typically purchase the one I've researched that meets all my requirements. Then I am fastidious with the care and keeping of that car. Typically a car isn't any kind of investment—it can depreciate rather quickly—but when I keep my cars clean and in mint condition, I have found I can sharply decrease that rate of depreciation. I have even had a few occasions where I broke even or even gained a profit. Now, that's the limit of my financial advice, since it's nowhere near my field of expertise. Suffice to say, I learned these things from my dad.

He worked hard every day of the week, but every year, for at least two weeks, along with certain long weekends or days off, my father would show us the benefit of that "work hard, play hard" principle. To this day, all us kids remember the vacations that resulted in significant family times simply because my parents had saved for them. We remember how fun it was in the fall to go with my dad on a Saturday off, up north and out of the city by about an hour to the apple-cider mill to get some fresh-squeezed Michigan apple cider. Even after a long week of work for him and school and work for us, we would all pile into the car almost every Saturday night, run by the McDonalds (a new thing for my generation), and pick up our nineteen-cent hamburgers and fries. Then we'd take the food to the park, eat together, and play at the park together.

A few years later, I worked at a restaurant called Blazo's on the east side of Detroit. Blazo's was known for their pies, and I found it so much fun to bring home to the family a full pie of some sort each Saturday after work. It would be my contribution to the Sunday dinner! I paid for it with my earnings (although, I did get an employee discount). That's a powerful feeling of accomplishment and contribution! Doing things like that still motivates me to this day. From this and other scenarios involving this particular principle, I learned the importance of serving versus being served. I think a large majority of our teen-agers today could use this lesson, big time! (Did that just make me sound old?)

Shirley Says

In between the working and playing, have you ever had a child come up to you and utter the words "I'm bored"? I have to admit, that was the one phrase that triggered me the worst during those parenting years. We had a huge amount of games, puzzles, books, bikes, roller skates, and bats and balls, yet they still were bored. So one day, to make sure I never heard that phrase again, I determined to find a remedy. The very next time I heard those words uttered, I replied enthusiastically, "Great! These two rooms need the baseboards dusted, the windows at the back of the house need cleaning inside and out, and the basement steps need to be swept and then mopped." After making sure all chores were completed to my satisfaction, the child (or children) would escape as fast as they could, and I wouldn't hear those words for a week or two. Problem solved!

I came to realize that I was keeping them in a clean home, clean clothes, and clean underwear, and additionally, I fed and watered them. I did not feel it was in my job description to entertain them as well. They needed to learn to do that themselves. We planned many fun times as a family throughout the year, as well as a usual two-week vacation in the summers, but they had to eventually realize that they were responsible for their own contentment. Once they did, I didn't hear that phrase "I'm bored" very often anymore.

Work Ethics

There is another part of this "work hard, play hard" principle that should be addressed here. I didn't realize the dynamic until I was a father with my own teenagers in the home. My wife and I used to have what seemed to be continuous fights with our son, Luke, to get him to do his chores. Mowing the lawn, taking out the trash, even picking up his clothes and doing some laundry were usually meet with "I will, I promise," but nothing would be done.

Finally, my wife had it with him. She told him if he didn't pick up his clothes and put them in the laundry hamper, she wasn't going to do any more washing of his dirty clothes. In fact, she informed him that any clothes of his left on the floor or around the house would be collected by her and thrown away or given away. That commonsense approach worked really great when, within about eleven days, he got out of the shower and had no more clothes to put on. What a shock for him! Since we didn't reside in a nudist colony, he suddenly got the point. He thought all his clothes were gone to the nearby Goodwill store, but my wife had just stuck them all in a big plastic trash bag and hid them in the garage where he couldn't find them. She did not give them back to him, however, simply hoping the lesson was learned. She knew better. Instead, she made him buy back all the clothes she had collected with his earned money. Yep, even his underwear. Can you imagine how galling it has to be to buy back your dirty underwear? Now the lesson was learned! By the way, years later when Luke was first living in Denver and was the master of his own apartment, I happened to visit him for an overnight visit. I had stopped in Denver following a long day of meetings and travel, and I was beat. Sitting with him that night in the living room of his tiny apartment I looked around and realized how neat and tidy he now kept it. I took pride in knowing we'd had a small part to play in the high standards he had set for himself. Unknowingly, after my long day, I slipped off my shoes, then removed my socks and stuck them into my shoes. I watched him. He watched me, composed himself for a few moments, and then with all serious asked me if I planned on leaving my shoes "in the middle of the apartment like that?" He'd trashed my house most of his childhood and teen years, and here I sat with my shoes and socks next to me in the chair I was sitting in, and you'd think I had just committed the unpardonable sin.

Sarah Says

At our house, work begins at a young age. But it's not a punishment or slavery-type situation. Our kids love it and look so forward to the day that they are assigned their own "zone." In our home, every child is on one major duty for a year or even two. This gives them a chance to master their task. So a four-year-old may be given the zone of helping an older sibling empty the dishwasher. They are on that zone for a year or two and really learn how to do it well. Then they are promoted to another zone. Our older children are used to this system and, once they have cycled through every zone in the house, I give them the freedom to let me know what zone they prefer the most and stick mostly with that. But the good thing is that by the time they hit their teen years, they know how to clean off the table after a meal, how to sweep the floors and take out the trash, how to clean off the counters and put the food away, how to rinse the dishes and load the dishwasher, how to wash the pots and pans, and how to do the laundry. Not only do they know how, but they are good at it! Another beauty of this system is that there are no charts or graphs or complicated systems that involve a lot of sibling arguments regarding who is doing what chore on what day and for what meal. Sometime in their teen years, they settle into areas that they like the best and help train younger children. But by the age of thirteen, I have each child taking care of their own laundry from start to finish, and it is not even intimidating for them. They have done laundry for eight or ten people in the past—washing, drying, folding, and putting away clothes for one is *no sweat*. Likewise, I believe this will help them as they transition out of our home into caring for homes of their own.

Our kids also have one room they are in charge of besides their own bedroom. This means when we do a quick clean-up of the house once or twice a day, they head to that room (including the backyard) and make sure everything is tidy and back in its place. Does our house get messy? Absolutely! We are thirteen people who can destroy a house in about thirteen minutes. But it also can return to tidy very quickly and at least be manageable. Everyone appreciates the house when it is cleaned up. Even the youngest children tend to play better when their toys are not scattered to every corner of the house. When I am looking around the house and feeling overwhelmed at the state of affairs, I often remind myself to gather everyone together so we can quickly do what would alone take me several hours to accomplish. After that, we can relax and have all the fun. Playing hard is a priority and important in so many ways, but it comes after the work is done.

When it comes to teaching your children a strong work ethic, I would highly suggest you act just as a good boss should and would act toward your child one day. Get that teenager used to the understanding that what is expected of them will be inspected. In our current culture, where sports have the "everyone is a winner no matter the score" mantra and where the schools seemingly continue to downgrade their requirements so no child is "left behind," the real world environment hasn't changed much at all. Employers still have tasks and expectations of their employees. An employer is still going to expect that task to be completed on time and with excellence. That employee is still going to receive at least one yearly performance review or evaluation, and they are still going to earn a wage and receive increases in wage and benefits based on how well they do their job.

That future employee, future husband, or future wife will learn all those valuable skills right now, in your home. Skip this step and you will set your children up for failure, pure and simple. But do your due diligence in this area and they will make you so very proud of their conduct and abilities. It won't matter at all what they choose to do in life, but it will matter to you that they are doing it to the best of their ability. You'll be able to say, just like I now say, "That's my boy," or "That's my girl."

By the way, as a side note should you be interested, when it came time for each of our children to pick their mates, I noticed they each picked people just like them—people with a strong work ethic and a desire to do and be their best. There was no way my daughter was going to marry a deadbeat for a husband, and my son wasn't interested in marrying someone who didn't have the very same degree of satisfaction of a job well done as he did.

Here's one more thing about the work ethic you need to know so you're not caught off guard or disappointed in some way when you ask your child to do some work for you around the house. Almost invariably, no matter what that teenager is doing for a job, whether it leads to a career or not, whatever the pay might even be, they are going to work their backsides off for a boss that isn't you. You might be tempted to take this as a slight, or even a sign of disrespect. Don't. Our human nature is such that we respond really well in environments where our talents, abilities, and work is noticed and appreciated by someone who doesn't know us or doesn't live in the same house as we do. In fact, even if you own a family business and your dream is one day for your son or daughter to join you in that business, they are going to be a better employee or employer if they've had an opportunity to work for someone other than you. They will learn and form their own opinion through that experience. They will learn what makes for a good employee and a good boss or a bad employee or a bad boss. I've seen both kinds in my lifetime and in every field where I ever worked. Learning the principle of a strong work ethic contributed in a large part to what made me a diligent and consistent employee—the kind someone wants to hire. That same work ethic taught me precisely what makes for a good boss and employer—the kind someone wants to work for. No bragging, just fact. This paradigm, in addition to what your child learns under your roof regarding work ethics, responsibility, accountability, and reward, will be the best formula for success your child could ever have. Your encouragement and involvement is a key. Someone else's encouragement and involvement in shaping your child in this area is even a bigger key.

The Reward of a Job Well Done Is Its Own Fulfillment

I can't tell you the number of times I have watched a parent seek to make their son or daughter into something that is actually the parent's dream, without ever considering the child might have diametrically opposed passions to those of Mom or Dad. Children need to be able to be directed and placed on their own unique journey and not on the journey you think they should be on, just because it's something you want for them. Here's where you need to engage in some real, down-to-earth common sense. As a father, you may look at that young seven-year-old boy and dream of the day he becomes another Michael Jordan for the NBA or the next Mickey Mantle of baseball fame. He may, indeed, like putting on a uniform and shagging ground balls around the baseball diamond or throwing three-pointers, but if he's not working at it or doesn't seem as interested in the game as you are, it's time to wise up. Ultimately, he will need his own fulfillment in this life and not be forced into fulfilling your dreams.

I have seen parents push all sorts of things on their children and, almost all the time, the push ends in disappointments, resentments, unfulfilled potential, or an outright rejection. Common sense should tell you that, as they mature, you not only get to know your child and their likes, dislikes, passions, and dreams as fully as possible, but then you find ways to affirm, reinforce, and accentuate those dreams for them. I can't tell you how many parents I've seen who have insisted that their children will all attend college "because I never could." Yet, you might have a child who attends but never latches on to any particular field of study. They end up at the end of four years without direction, without realized goals, without any sense of accomplishment or fulfillment, and with a huge educational debt. Perhaps you totally missed the fact that this particular child loved to get their hands dirty rebuilding automobile engines or enjoyed making a yard "pop" due to some brilliantly insightful landscaping techniques. Maybe, just maybe, college wasn't the path they needed to be on, but they went on that path because that was *your* dream.

On the other hand, I have witnessed teens who get it in their mind they're going to lead a band like Chicago or play guitar like Eric Clapton. Yet, all they've accomplished is to gather a couple of friends who like to also play and sing and make a lot of noise in your basement. If that teen is really serious with their musical passion and they dream of being "something significant" in that particular field one day, you're going to have to walk the balance beam of encouragement and excellence. The goal is to become the best, and if the goal is that level of achievement, then "good" is not good enough. You will need to point them to areas of study that will enlarge that talent and dream—things that will take work on their part. The group Chicago is a prime example of guys with a great dream who applied themselves diligently to their craft. They didn't just learn how to strum three or four chords in the key of E on the electric guitar or how to hammer out a cool riff on the bass. Nope. You listen to these guys talk. They know the music theory, music history, and musical arranging that is needed to make the kind of sound they make. They've learned what instruments sound best together. They know how the vocals should be arranged to grab the listener's ear. They have studied orchestral arrangements and have sought to expand on what others have done in this field. They can even tell you what others in their chosen field are doing at any given time. And they practiced, practiced, practiced. Only after all of this were they able to showcase their skills.

Whether your child is destined to become a physicist or an electrician, an accountant or a musician, learning to take pride in their field through hard work, study, and applying themselves is a feeling that cannot ever be reproduced by anything else. It's a sense of total fulfillment. I suppose it's even what a mother or father feels after some twenty or twenty-four years of intense parenting. Pride in a job well done. A "mission accomplished" moment.

Right now, though, you may be right in the middle of those teenage years and you're going crazy running all around chasing all sorts of "dreams" or helping them explore and formulate their passions. Can I make a suggestion? It doesn't take trying out every single sport, musical instrument, or other extracurricular activity to know whether they are naturally gifted in those arenas. My parents knew I wasn't gifted at sports by the time I was about seven years old. I played touch football in the street with the neighbors as a child, but even at seven, you could always find me with a book in my hand or at the library. I loved riding my bike up to the library. That was my summer enjoyment. I also excelled pretty well at the piano and took lessons from the ages of six to sixteen. I quit the lessons then, but years later I went back and took lessons from the concertmistress (principal pianist) of the Detroit Symphony for a couple of years. During high school, I also showed an aptitude to messing with electrical stuff, and I worked for quite a while with a man who taught me a lot about fixing televisions in his television repair shop. (This was in the days of the cathode ray tubes—look it up if you don't know about that.) I ended up going to a tech school and working on a degree in computer engineering after high school. When I finished that school, I got a job with Burroughs Computer Company in Detroit. It wasn't until I was in my early thirties that I went back and got a bachelor's in theology, then later my master of divinity and, finally, a doctor of ministry degree. Yes, I returned to my first love of reading, studying, writing, and communication. The same passion that was there when I was seven. Although it took quite a few years to progress to where I am today, the journey has been great and challenging, and all my jobs in that journey have brought a certain sense of satisfaction and fulfillment to me.

So what was the most important thing? I was encouraged and challenged by my parents and later by others, including my wife, every step of the way. I didn't let any obstacles stop me or create an impenetrable barrier, and I didn't let the naysayers (and they're always around, even at times in my own head) distract me from my goals to become the best I could possibly be. I learned early on in my home as a child that hard work could produce some fantastically satisfying results and also creates some great "play hard" moments. I learned how to press through to completion of a "thing" and how to approach everything I do with pride in a job well done.

I came across this quote a few years ago by a fellow named David O. McKay that I thought would be a good way to end this chapter. He said, "Let us realize that: the privilege to work is a gift, the power to work is a blessing, and the love of work is success."

Commonsense Application

- What kind of work ethic were you raised with? How has that affected teaching a strong work ethic to your children?
- What reward do you get, even now, in work, play, or hobby? Do your children know that you get fulfillment in these areas, and how?
- Do you tend to do things for your children in order to save them from hard work? Do you finish their homework for them? Do you give them what they need when they need it?
- Have you helped them establish a budget for their lives and shown them basic money management tools?

There are two gifts we should give our children. One is roots, and the other is wings.

—Unknown

CHAPTER EIGHT

"The Nest Isn't Empty Yet"

The Principle of Letting Go at the Right Time

Unexpectedly

The news was unexpected. My son, Luke, was working at the Lincoln airport for United Airlines, which, at the time, was flying mainline jets in and out of Lincoln. He had been working for them for about two years when the news came that United was going to downsize Lincoln to regional jet service. When this happens, employees are let go by United Airlines. Those who are lucky and qualify are hired by the new regional carrier. It usually means less pay, fewer benefits, and very little chance for advancement.

Luke was still living at home at the time. It was wonderful having him around as he made his own way in the world, helping out tremendously in various areas in the church I was pastoring, including the music department, with his great musical talent and abilities. Our daughter Sarah was still home, but in a bit of a transition herself at this time. Everything was going just great. Then this news came about United. When Luke told us, he included most of the details I just shared here, then stated, "Well, I guess that's the end of that job."

"Not so fast," I said. "Let me ask you some questions." Then I began to probe. When was the change going into effect, and how many more days did he have to work? What else did the executives have to say when they made the announcement? What did he think he should do? How well did he like United and his job with them?

Well, along about question two, I found out United was offering some employees—those they wanted to retain—the ability to transfer to a hub of United, most likely Chicago or Denver. Cautiously, and after taking a deep, silent gulp of air, I asked Luke if he would consider transferring to Denver. I knew something his mother was even not willing to admit— the time might have come for him to move out and get on with his life. Rather selfishly, I was hoping he would say, "No way, Dad. I want to continue living here and helping you with the music at the church. I can find another job." But I noticed by his look as I asked that question that he had been thinking, if ever so slightly, about what moving to Denver might look like. So over the course of the next several days as he and I talked, and I offered him my full support—help with relocation, finding an apartment to rent, and calming his mother down—he began to warm to the idea with increasing speed.

By the time a week or so had passed, he had put in his notice to United that he desired a transfer to Denver. They okayed the move. That was the start of his true career, his eventual meeting of his future wife, and his separation from us, his parents, after twenty years of living at home. The change was a bit scary for all of us, although I knew better than to let him feel or see any nervousness on my part.

I knew his move would bring the greatest amount of success and fulfillment to him—mostly because I had done the same thing at his age. Recently he celebrated his twenty-third anniversary of working for United, but even if he'd chosen not to stay with them, I knew this was the right move for Luke and the right timing for us. The church would find someone else to cover his responsibilities. The house would be a bit more lonely without his energy and laughter, and his mother and I would enter a new season and a different dynamic.

I also knew Luke was at a good place emotionally and was exhibiting great maturity and wise decision-making. I also knew we had done a pretty good job of raising him with a set of values and disciplines that would ensure he was in the best position to make a major life change. Denver was only about seven hours down the road by car. If ever needed, I could easily be available to him with support and counsel. Finally, I wanted his move out of our house to be a positive change for him. In other words, I didn't say to him, "You need to get out now. You're the right age, and your mother and I need the room," or some other negative or hurtful comment that would make our home somehow off-limits to him forevermore. In fact, my pastor's wife once gave Susan and me some very wise advice. She said, "Always leave the door unlocked for your children, and let them know it's unlocked." In other words, never let your children feel that your parent-child relationship is over; it has just changed into a new season.

All scary stuff, but necessary. After all, it's life!

Balancing Your Parental Role

A day like this comes for every parent, but for so many parents who have wrapped their lives up in raising their children, the "move out" can prove to be a difficult, if not an almost impossible, proposition to fathom.

I can't tell you how many parents I counseled as pastor who quit parenting way too early. Some would use the excuse that they really only "liked" the babies or elementary-age children, and they really didn't understand or enjoy the high school ages. And "God forbid if we want to be involved with them after they graduate from high school."

Most figured that once the child turned eighteen, that was the extent of the time they had committed to, and the parenting contract had now been concluded. Their children, in their estimation, needed to get on, get out, and figure out their lives for themselves. (More on this in a moment.)

More rarely, other parents simply couldn't let go. Often these parents wanted to continue to control the child, because somehow, "This child is just not ready to face the challenges of life." As I drilled down into their reasons for making such statements, I found that control was often a big issue for them. For example, they might have found it difficult to let their child work outside the home. They may have resisted allowing them to take the car or go anywhere alone (if they even allowed that child to obtain a driver's license). They hovered over every conversation and relationship the child ever attempted to have, always putting their two cents in.

In some cases, these kinds of parents were very insecure about the way they had raised their child up to that point, feeling inadequate in properly preparing them for adult life. Perhaps they felt they hadn't instilled the necessary values and decision-making skills necessary to mature.

Other cases, more shocking and sad for me as the family's pastor and a friend, involved insecurity resulting in envy or jealousy of the child. Sometimes parents were jealous of the child's ability to leave and start something new and exciting when the parents weren't able to do so. These parents reasoned that if the child were to move on, they could actually do better, be more successful, make more money, or somehow achieve so much more than the parent had ever done. This type of control was not looking out for the child, but looking out for the parents' own selfish interests.

I had to ask myself, "What kind of father doesn't want his son to be more successful and more fulfilled than he was?" or

"What kind of mother would not want to see her daughter happy, content, popular, or fruitful?" I would shake my head and feel so sorry for that particular child, because I knew they would always approach life going forward in secret so as not to stir up the jealousy of the parent. Or they would always hold back in life, family, and career in order to not make the parent feel less-than.

Other parents lean on their children for their own emotional support. A lot of underlying issues can cause this dynamic. Perhaps the parents' marriage is bad or failing, and a mother looks to a particular child to supply the emotional help that the spouse no longer supplies. In the case of a single parent, those feelings may even seem justified. Sometimes in a single-parent home (but not limited to that paradigm) the departure of an only child or the last child can be particularly wrenching. That child is not only loved but has been a companion of sorts, and most certainly has received more focused attention due to the absence of another parent, either physically or emotionally.

Shirley Says

Several years ago we arrived at a new milestone in our parenting. All our children were grown, or at least they looked like they were, but they were still our "kids." Right?

Are they really ready to take full responsibility for the major decisions they will be making going forward? Probably not, we figured, but although they lacked the experience we knew would help them, they were ready, and we had raised them with a great level of self-confidence.

When you reach this level of parenting, you will transition from these people just being your children to their being good friends whom you will enjoy talking to and listening to their dreams for their lives and their futures.

In spite of their bravado, they will still seek your approval on some major decisions. I think instinctively they know it's a walk through a minefield at times. Even though they have the confidence, they know down deep they lack the necessary experience.

It was during this stage that we found the best way to direct them is to ask more questions rather than supplying them with answers. Those questions produce wonderful and significant dialogue. Typically, a very important moment would occur in the conversation when they finally asked for our opinion. We learned to never offer that opinion too quickly or prematurely but to wait patiently for that right moment when they ask. When they ask, they are telling you they're ready to receive.

Don't make the mistake of thinking they don't want your direction or opinion. They do! They also want your approval. They just want it on their timeline and not yours. Plus, they'll never let you know they are not quite as confident about things as they make out to be. In other words, what their mouth might be saying is not what is fully in their heart.

So, in the final analysis, parenthood doesn't end with the grown children leaving the nest. Being a parent is just the start of a new level of relationship with the people you know more intimately than anyone else.

I can guarantee your phone will ring with questions or comments or the solicitation of advice the moment their first child is born. That right there is when the reward finally comes—grandchildren. All that hard work, patient endurance, and frustrations are wiped away in a moment when you experience the joy of grandchildren, and now, for us, great-grandchildren.

This potential moving out and away on the part of that child can stir up fears of loneliness, loss, and losing out. If not addressed with balance, these feelings can become almost overwhelming and debilitating to that parent.

What a horrible family dynamic those unchecked and unconfronted attitudes and points of view can make.

Now, again, I was thankful that I didn't encounter this "not willing to let go" paradigm too often, but I did encounter it enough to realize and learn that, for myself and my children, I wanted the very best and most success for them. Also, I watched my father exhibit this mindset toward us three boys. I wanted my children to know that, no matter what they did, I would always be a parent who would support them and look for ways to affirm their choices. With that type of relationship commitment, I also knew that if, on occasion, I couldn't affirm a decision—particularly the more critical ones—I would enjoy the open door and ability to let them know my thoughts, without requiring them to do what I said. It was still being a good parent, but now that the kids were older, I was parenting under a different set of rules and balance.

Quitting Too Early

I said previously I would come back to this particular aspect of parenting our children in their later teen years. I am convinced, in my own case and in talking with other friends and colleagues, that my wife and I did more parenting—more intense, more complicated, more critical—of our children between the ages of seventeen to twenty-four then we did for the first seventeen years combined.

I thought the baby and toddler years, with all their diaper bags, car seats, nighttime crying, and nonexistent or extremely limited communication skills, were the hardest thing anyone could be expected to endure. Even the terrible twos and threes and fours, fives, and sixes weren't as intense. Junior high, with all its erupting emotions, hormones, and nasty little snooty and cliquish girls in my daughter's seventh-grade class? That was a breeze. Even worrying about Luke driving the car past the curfew hour when I'd told him to be home, with me pacing the family room with my phone ready to press 911, was a cakewalk compared to those years between seventeen and twenty-four.

Think about it. These are the years when so much of life and its corresponding decisions are happening in your child's life. And these are just the normal day-to-day decisions, like, "Should I take a job at Burger King or McDonalds?" or "Should I date Thelma or Louise this Friday night?"

At this age, the choice of vocational education or perhaps college education, multiple job opportunities (you hope), and whom you're getting serious about dating increase the simple questions to a much more critical level. These questions now become "life decisions."

More of these "life decisions" are made during the ages of seventeen and twenty-four than at any other time during a child's life, even if they live to be one hundred. The reason these decisions are so critical, and why I refer to them as "life decisions," is that we fail to realize the typical child has had no experiences up to this point that have taught him or her how to make these life-changing decisions. After all, experience is a wonderful teacher, and you as a parent have had a lot more experience than the child.

Here's the problem with that. By the time children reach the seventeen- or eighteen-year-old mark, they think they are more than capable of making these critical "life decisions." Now, you and I know they have no factual basis for thinking that, much less believing it, but that doesn't concern them. They're out to prove you wrong. In fact, science tells us that boys' brains aren't even fully developed until the age of twenty-five or so. And unless they actually ask you, "What do you think about this or that?" (and you should never ever ignore that question, ever), you are going to have to find a way, creatively, to offer your commonsense advice or input without treating them as if they're fourteen or younger.

Let me offer you an example of some interface I had with my daughter Sarah during this critical time period in her life. When Sarah was around fifteen, we began to explore what she might want to do with her life. She excelled in her schoolwork and grades, and she displayed an admirable maturity and common sense for her age. We also saw what she was interested in by what she was reading or talking about. In other words, she was starting to dream about her future.

All of that was pretty encouraging, so around the dinner table or other one-on-one times, we would talk to her about those dreams. We knew to listen very closely without too much comment in order to really hear her heart and get a sense of how her thinking was developing. As we probed and asked significant questions, in due time, she was able to formulate, then articulate, the idea that she wanted to live in a "mission-field environment" or a Third World country, be married, and have children . . . lots of children.

Well, I could tell that I was hearing her heart and passion regarding this plan, but of course, her vision was still very broad and without much detail. I suppose a lot of people want to leave the comforts of their own home and culture and move to a foreign land to help people and make an impact (in Sarah's case, bringing the love of Jesus Christ to the unreached). By the way, she came by it naturally. Her mother was raised in Nigeria, and her mother's parents had served the bulk of their lives in both Kenya and Nigeria. So I totally got where she was coming from, but I also had enough travel experience in those parts of the world to know that the missionary paradigm of her grandparents' years had changed drastically. These days, you couldn't just go to Kenya, raise a family, and preach or teach the Bible on weekends to people living in the bush, since most countries issue visas based on what you can contribute to the good of the whole country.

I decided, however, to feed her passion a bit before offering any obstacles or roadblocks. I liked how Sarah was thinking, and we thought her dream fit well to her personality and giftings. I promised to take her with me on my next overseas trip. I had a three-week journey coming up in about nine months that involved going to Bulgaria, then down to Kenya. I suggested she start saving for it.

Now, before you jump me for making her pay for her plane ticket, I actually felt that this would be the more commonsense thing to do. First, it would prove to me and her mom that the passion and desire were genuine and not just a passing fantasy, where the only by-product was going overseas and having a great time. Second, I wanted to see if she was willing to count the cost and really adjust her priorities, to set herself up to make the trip significant.

Guess what? She did both! She had been saving for a car, but she diverted all that saved money, plus collected even more, in order to go with me. She figured she could save for the car at another time, and she would borrow mine or her mom's when she needed transportation. That she did this was remarkable to me, only because I'm not sure I could have done the same thing about *anything* I was passionate about at that age.

She began to research and study about the areas we would be visiting. She also spoke to a ton of her friends and relatives, and most importantly to us, about it. She began to pray about this trip. She was serious! Her passion was real, and her dream was alive.

We went on the trip and had a great time. We hung out together for three weeks in all sorts of situations with different potential culture shocks, but it seemed as natural as breathing air to Sarah. I saw she flourished under very different culture paradigms, which gave her an appetite for more. I could tell we were on the right path. However—and I knew ahead of time this would happen—she observed that just being a wife, mom, and missionary in Kenya was not going to translate well in that country. Things had changed dramatically since the 1950s and '60s when her grandpa and grandma had served there.

When we got home, after the initial flush of a trip well done, we were able to sit down and begin to put some meat to the bones of Sarah's passions. As we looked at this future with her, we understood she was going to need a skill in order to have something to take to a foreign country that would make her valuable to those she would serve, as well as valuable to herself, no matter where God directed her footsteps.

After much discussion, we came down to either getting a teaching degree or a nursing degree. With the same intensity, she began to investigate those two avenues, finally settling on nursing. She knew that going forward with this plan might delay her timing a bit before she could actually live out the dream of going overseas, but her diligence, along with our support and affirmation, let her know that although the dream might be delayed a bit—what person her age doesn't want everything they do to happen immediately?— it didn't mean that "delay" meant "never."

Sarah Says

I remember being very sick of school when I finished high school. Further education was not something I was even remotely interested in pursuing at that moment. I loved how my parents helped me narrow my options down to two and pick between them: teaching or nursing. However, I have vivid memories of my parents discussing with me the benefits of going back to school and getting a degree that could be very useful and open doors for me overseas. I remember going into nursing school not really excited about the whole venture, but I did know that I was making the right decision. Sort of the way my pre-schoolers do so much better picking out their own clothes when I narrow their options down to two. My parents did not force me into those options, but approached the conversations in a way that felt very helpful and guiding, not demanding or directing. I am very thankful that I do not have regrets in regard to my college education and the time that took. I am also grateful I did not have a lot of debt that was hard to pay off, considering I did not work for many years before deciding to stay home and take care of my babies! I believe my parents considered that when helping guide my decisions, as I really wanted marriage and motherhood above any career.

After three years of nursing school, Sarah worked for a season overseas in Kenya, as well as a season with a local hospital and GP office, until one day I came home with the news that a friend's parents operated an orphanage for abandoned girls in Coimbatore, India. It was a six-month gig.

I asked, "Would you be interested in going?"

I knew the answer before the question was even asked. The dreams and the passion were coming together for Sarah, and she would soon be on her way to her own life and destiny. I must have been crazy for letting her go, though. When we chatted by phone that first Christmas Day of her overseas venture, we could hear a great deal of loneliness in her voice. It took every amount of willpower not to pull out the AMEX card, book the ticket, and leave that very day for India!

By the way, during her stint in Kenya before India, Sarah had met a tall, dark, handsome guy named Solomon Mwania (Solo). We didn't think much of it at the time. He was just a passing fancy, a small fling of the heart. Boy, was I wrong. But that's another story for another time.

Close Encounters of the Good Kind

Can I offer some very practical and commonsense advice on how you can positively approach this most important season in the life of your child? Remember, your role will have to change—perhaps as much change as your child is experiencing. Don't disengage. Don't put it off for another time and, whatever you do, don't quit on your child too early. You have to remain available and interested at all times.

I can think of four things you might want to consider during this time in your child's life:

1. *Know your child.* It dismays me to ask parents what their child wants to do in life or what educational path they are looking to follow, and their response is "I don't know." What? You should be the first person to

know, or at least have an inkling of an idea. Though at times your kids may appear and act as if they don't want you to know anything, don't give in to that attitude, because it's a total lie! I haven't met a child approaching that young-adult age yet who doesn't want to talk about themselves. Let that ego open the door for you to engage in significant conversation. Besides, you'll be surprised at what you learn. This means you're going to have to . . .

2. *Ask the right questions.* With my daughter Sarah, the wrong questions would have been, "You're getting to the age where you need to decide what you're going to do. So what are you going to do?" or "How soon do you think you'll be moving out of the house?" or "How do you think you're going to possibly live overseas and do that?" "How do you think you're going to afford that?" "What about college? You have to go to college, you know." You get my point. Asking the right kinds of questions in the right way shows you're interested in finding out more about your child and what they're thinking (see number one on this list). At this point as a parent, you're looking for insight and nothing more. When you ask the question, don't be afraid of the answer. Some parents won't ask the question because they're afraid of what the answer might be. You're going to have to steel yourself to possibly hear an answer that, in your opinion and experience, might be totally undoable or off the wall. That's okay. You don't have to respond to everything immediately. First, what's the rush? They're typically not going to run off and do anything based on your initial conversation. Instead, look interested, act interested, *be*

interested, and let your face and eyes show you are listening and are very interested in what they're saying. Which leads me to my next point.

3. *Keep your opinions to yourself (for now).* At this stage and level of parenting, it's really not your opinion they're after. They really want to know if you are interested, and if, going forward, they can include you in future talks about future plans. In other words, it's a test. Don't fail the test by putting in your two cents in an inappropriate place or time! You'll run the risk of ruining future conversations and interchanges. Remember, if you're not listening closely to them, they will find someone else who will. That someone else might be someone you don't want them engaging with regarding such serious life decisions, probably because those people might hold values that differ from yours. It's critical at this point to think in the long-term about your relationship with your child. Short-term is junior-high stuff. This is a whole different ball game. You're not only wanting to engage with them at this stage in their life but are actually setting up a future paradigm where they will engage with you when they're married and in their twenties, thirties, forties, and beyond. You will have modeled for them the way your relationship will look going forward. If it's successful at this point, they will assume it will remain so going forward. I have pretty much learned to only offer my opinion when I am specifically asked the question by one of my children, "Dad, what do you think?" Even then, I usually follow it up with my own question: "Do you really want to know what I think?" (You can smile here.)

4. *Make yourself available and help their dreams come to life.* This can take on several forms, but once you've had at least one—but not limited to one—conversation where you have fully heard their dreams, plans, and passions, then look for ways, using all your resources, to help make that dream happen. This might include calling your friend or brother who works, or knows someone who works, in the field your child wants to enter and arranging a chat, or finding someone willing to let your child shadow them at work for a day. A mentorship might then be established that will not only enhance your child's dreams and career but will be a living example of what they can become to someone else in the future. Or it might mean, as in my case, arranging for my daughter to come with me on an overseas trip, helping her find and enroll in a nursing school, then helping to find a way to go overseas and practice that skill set—just as she envisioned herself doing one day. Trust me, you'll hate to see her travel halfway across the world alone, but at the same time, you'll be so proud that you had a hand in making her dreams come true.

Becoming a Life Coach and Living with Balance

I hinted at this in the previous section. In my opinion, frequently parents think way too much in the short-term. I totally get that and am guilty of the same. Every time we left the house for anything—church, family visits, doctor's appointments—with our babies (Luke and Sarah were only nineteen months apart), we seemed to pack up half the house. We carried all that stuff out to the car and packed the car a certain way to fit it all in, then drove to our destination, where we would then unpack the stuff and carry it all into the church, other people's homes, or doctor's offices. Once the time there was completed, we would reverse the whole process to get ourselves back home. We did this in rain, shine, snow, sleet, and hail. I know you get what I'm saying.

Well, I viewed this as short-term maneuvering. I would beg God for it to end so I wouldn't have to mess with all this "stuff," though, at the time, it felt like it was going to be for the rest of eternity. If I hadn't thought short-term, I would have lost it on more than one occasion. Thankfully, it came to an end one day. Little did I know about another short-term season called "toddlers."

Here's my point. By the time your son or daughter has reached that seventeen-year-old mark, things are going to change with regard to your parent/child relationship. The discipline and punishment phase is winding down, the "making them do their chores" is just about over, and certainly their primary education, whether that's parochial, governmental, or homeschooling-based, is also winding down.

Think back to when you were going through this season yourself as a seventeen- or eighteen-year-old. It was thrilling, scary, challenging, and overwhelming. You were moving into a new role as a full-fledged adult. And while everyone matures at a different pace, you still hit the same marks everyone experiences at some point or another. This is the point, you might remember, where you needed a parent or another strong influence in your life, more than ever. However, you needed that relationship at a different dynamic than when you were younger. I can guarantee your child will be feeling the exact same thing.

The way your relationship will look for the rest of your life, and theirs, will hinge on what happens during these critical years. If you quit too early, you will lose out on helping them with some of the most important decisions they will ever make. If you won't let go, but attempt to keep them under your roof and under your control, you will drive them out with a bad taste in their mouth.

I can say that Susan and I enjoy a wonderful relationship with both of our children now. We also enjoy the same relationship with their spouses. We were even asked our input on whom they chose to marry and were blessed to affirm their choices. And now, we love having great and growing relationships with our thirteen grandchildren. (This number may have changed by the time you are reading this book.)

By the way, let me offer you some hope and promise. It is now a blast for us to watch our children raise their children as they move through the stages of parenting, just as we did. They're all doing a great job, that's for sure, but it's fun to watch the differences between the two households. There are nuanced things that each do differently than we did. This is probably a result of saying to themselves, "When we have children, we're not going to do it the way our parents did." However, we still see the same values, the same open communication, and the same sense of mutual honor in both homes. That is so very cool.

But the best benefit, by far, is being able to enjoy the relationships with all those grands without having to parent them! Besides, I'm too old for all that again.

Commonsense Applications
- How well do you really know your children? Can you identify their passions, dreams, and talents? Do they know you know?
- When was the last time you sat down for a one-to-one with that middle teenager or older child and had a serious

talk about the future? Do you try to avoid this type of discussion? Why?

- If asked, would your teenager say they feel you're "in their corner" when to comes to their future plans? Are you able to talk dreams as well as reality in the same conversation? Have you been a resource for them?

The greatest legacy one can pass on to one's children, grandchildren, and great-grandchildren is not money or other material things accumulated in one's life, but rather a legacy of character and faith.

—Billy Graham

CHAPTER NINE

Will It Ever End?

"Will it ever end?" is a question that has been asked by every parent regarding raising children since Adam and Eve had two boys named Cain and Abel. That question is usually followed quickly by, "Can you take my kids for a day (or a week, month, year, forever) and make them change?"

Even with just one child, I wondered if "it" would ever end. Every time we left the house, we took half the house with us, or so it seemed. Bottles, diapers, change of clothes times two, diaper bags, baby carrier, stroller, and on and on. The list was endless. But now, having lived through the raising of children myself, I can tell you those years went by so fast, I can hardly remember some of the more important details.

Did my wife and I feel constantly tired? You bet. Did we experience frustrations and exasperation? Again, you'd better believe it. Did we ever want to return them from wherever they came from? Well, I thought it a few times, but I'm not sure Susan would admit to it. Are we glad we had children? Absolutely!

To answer the question I've posed, the hands-on job of parenting does end at some point, whether good, bad, or indifferent. We all want it to end well, and we'll look at what that might mean in a moment. Sometimes it doesn't end well, and that too needs to be faced. The more difficult result is experienced when a child is raised by a parent or parents with an indifferent, "I don't care" mindset or attitude.

I have met these types of parents and I have to admit, I don't understand them at all. Some take a totally hands-off approach to parenting, while others are so caught up in their own agenda, pursuits, and pleasures that they actually don't realize the children in their home are screaming for attention or input. When none is forthcoming, a multitude of reactions can result based on the personality of the given child. As a pastor, I've seen everything from total, complete, and unchecked rebellion to a hermit-recluse type of response on the part of children suffering from lack of parental input. This is probably the most dangerous and precarious way of parenting because it will lead to unpredictable extremes in the child's life. And should a child raised this way happen to have children of their own one day, without some sort of miracle and mid-course correction, they will repeat the mistakes of the original parent because they have not seen engaged parenting modeled.

In spite of your own career, personal goals, agenda, or desire to make everything in your life about you, at some point you will have to take responsibility for raising that child you brought into your home. You need to recognize both the gift and the tremendous opportunity you've been handed to affect generations beyond yourself.

Sometimes the parenting doesn't end well. I mentioned in chapter 5 that if you, as the parent, are dealing with unresolved conflicts in your emotions or attitudes, you will need to adjust or confront those areas before you can ever expect to parent and see a good and satisfying outcome in your children when they become adults.

The good news is, there are many of you who had a pretty horrible childhood or nonexistent parental influence, and yet you have found the strength and will to not only turn that around but have gone on to succeed in life as well as parenting. I have watched this transformation over and over again and stand amazed at the goodness of God when we set our minds and hearts to do right. Over the years as a pastor, I got to know my congregants pretty well. I was constantly awed by stories so foreign to my experience being raised in a hands-on, loving environment. Yet the individual or couple sitting across from me blew me away with their wisdom, their faith, their children and, yes, their ability to rise above all sorts of difficulties and traumas.

I used the term "will" a few sentences back, and I did so on purpose. We are each given a will by God that allows us to exercise a great deal of control and direction over how things will turn out for us. This will is a gift!

Although our will sometimes causes us to choose wrong, it can also cause us to choose very right. By observing good role models, we can exercise our will to do things differently in our parenting approach in spite of our background or personal negative experiences. By reading books (like this one) and dialoguing with others, we can adjust and reform our parenting skills to become better parents and role models. All is never lost.

Although I have largely refrained from making this book too spiritual or religious, I do want to tell you one thing: God wants you to succeed as a parent. He was the only truly successful (read: no mistakes) parent there has ever been or will be. The good news? He is cheering for your success. The key to that success is aligning your will to His.

It's like going to a lumberyard to purchase a ten-foot two-by-four. You want that board perfectly straight, without any bends or dips or marks that would make it unusable once you get it home. Eyeballing that board might make you think it's flawless. But the only possible way to ensure it is perfect is to align it with a board that is known to be perfect. Only then will you realize it wasn't nearly as straight and perfect as you'd thought. That's why alignment of our parenting to God's perfect parenting is so very important.

The three authors of this book aren't perfect models. We made mistakes. We took dips and turns in our journey that we wish we could do over again. We curved out to the left and right more times than we can count. Even though two of us no longer parent in our own home, we look back on certain experiences and wish we had done things differently. That's okay for us, and it's okay for you. Alignment is hard work, and we don't always get it right. But remember this: God is cheering you on toward success. All three of us want this book to encourage you, first and foremost, and then enlarge and envision your life going forward.

One more thing about this paradigm called "will." Not only do you have a free will; so do the children you are raising. You can align with God in your parenting. You can do the hard work of researching, educating, and resourcing yourself to become a better parent. You can sincerely want the very best for each child and equip them for successful adulthood the best you know how. But they also come with a will. They will eventually make their own choices about all sorts of things in life. They will decide for themselves whether to align with God when raising their own children, your grandchildren. They will decide for themselves which values you taught them to keep and which to reject (sometimes all of them). They will produce good fruit or bad based on their own choices and will. You can't circumvent their will, just as no one could ever circumvent yours, including God. He will never cross someone's will.

These kinds of decisions are hard to watch. We know. It's hard to accept some twenty-plus years of hard work and diligence thrown away with lousy decisions by our adult children. We get that. However, you must still keep doing your job as a parent, encourager, and cheerleader. Let each child know of your love for them and stand ready to pick up the pieces. Such is the life of a parent.

There is one wonderful, often overlooked promise given to us by God when we sincerely look to align with Him when raising our children. A seriously old proverb (22:6 in the NIV Bible) informs us that if we "start children off on the way they should go, and even when they are old they will not turn from it." As a pastor, I have seen this proverb play out countless times. However, it can really try your patience and your faith. Hang in there. Just do your job the best you can and leave the rest to God. He takes good care of that which we commit to His safekeeping.

Now let us leave you with something that will really make you think. In order to be born, you needed two parents, four grandparents, eight great-grandparents, sixteen second great-grandparents, thirty-two third great-grandparents, sixty-four fourth great-grandparents, 128 fifth great-grandparents, 256 sixth great-grandparents, 512 seventh great-grandparents, 1,024 eighth great-grandparents, and 2,048 ninth great-grandparents. For you to be born today from twelve previous generations you needed a total of 4,094 ancestors over four hundred years.

Now when you think about all the struggles, battles, and difficulties endured, how much sadness and happiness, you begin to realize how much was experienced to get you to this point in your life. When you think of all the love stories and how many expressions of hope for the future your ancestors had for you to be here, right now, in this moment of history, you realize so much more fully the significance of your life and influence into coming generations. So, the next time you question your reason for existence and wonder if you are the only one who struggles, just remember you have all these people watching over you. You were not only meant to be here; you were meant to be another key element in a long line of legacy, heritage, and tradition.

Notes

Introduction

1. Dictionary.com, s.v. "common sense," https://www.dictionary.com/browse/common-sense.

2. Etymology Dictionary, s.v. "common sense," https://etymology.en-academic.com/10083/common_sense.

2. "What Goes Around Comes Around": The Principle of Honor

1. Joseph Umidi, *Transformational Intelligence: Creating Cultures of Honor @ Home and Work* (Virginia Beach: Lifeforming Institute, 2014), 10.

2. Umidi, *Transformational Intelligence*, 12.

3. "Others May; You Cannot": The Importance of Values

1. L. P. Lebret, "Civilization Ceases," Forbes Quotes, https://www.forbes.com/quotes/author/r-p-lebret/.

2. John Adams, "From John Adams to Massachusetts Militia, 11 October 1798," National Archives, https://founders.archives.gov/documents/Adams/99-02-02-3102.

3. Harvey Mackay, "Values Determine Who We Are," *The Business Journals*, May 1, 2017, https://www.bizjournals.com/bizjournals/how-to/growth-strategies/2017/05/values-determine-who-we-are.html.

4. "Let the Punishment Fit the Crime": The Principle of Discipline

   1. Jeffrey Frank, *The Trials of Harry S. Truman* (New York: Simon & Schuster, 2022), 58.

5. "Guess Who Wet the Bed?": The Principle of Healthy Emotional Well-Being

   1. Daniel J. Siegel and Mary Hartzell, *Parenting from the Inside Out: How a Deeper Self-Understanding Can Help You Raise Children Who Thrive* (New York: Penguin Random House, 2013), 1–2.

   2. Coach John Wooden, "The Pyramid of Success," *Life@ Work GroupZine*, vol. 2 (Nashville: Thomas Nelson, 2006), 165–67.